PRAYING
WITH
DAVID

Honest Prayers
for Hard Seasons

PRAYING
WITH
DAVID

MARK BECTON

Foreword by Tony Merida

AMBASSADOR INTERNATIONAL
GREENVILLE, SOUTH CAROLINA & BELFAST, NORTHERN IRELAND
www.ambassador-international.com

PRAYING WITH DAVID

Honest Prayers for Hard Seasons
©2023 by Mark Becton
All rights reserved

Paperback ISBN: 978-1-64960-378-4
eISBN: 978-1-64960-382-1

Cover Design by Hannah Linder Designs
Interior Design by Dentelle Design
Edited by Martin Wiles

AMBASSADOR INTERNATIONAL
Emerald House
411 University Ridge, Suite B14
Greenville, SC 29601
United States
www.ambassador-international.com

AMBASSADOR BOOKS
The Mount
2 Woodstock Link
Belfast, BT6 8DD
Northern Ireland, United Kingdom
www.ambassadormedia.co.uk

The colophon is a trademark of Ambassador, a Christian publishing company.

APPRECIATION

THANK YOU TO ALL WHO encouraged me to publish this. Your affirmation often came at the right time. Thank you, Elaine Wilson. You were a treasured gift for eighteen years as my administrative assistant. Even after the Father changed both our assignments, you generously offered your time and eye to proof this.

And thank you, Loree. This is my fourth book. As with the previous three, I cannot write without inserting you into the pages. Watching you honestly and dependently follow Jesus forty years has shown me so much. To this day, God keeps using you to grow me.

Also, thank you, Redemption Hill Church. Your warm embrace, kind words, and generosity has made this publication possible. And to students of Grimke Seminary who took my course on "Prayer and the Man of God," your constant prodding to get this published helped me stay at it.

But above all, my greatest thanks is to You, Father. You have been patient and kind to me when I have been and often still am a brute beast before You. And Father, thank You for Your persistent care. I praise You when I see the comforting touch of Your rod and staff. And on the days I don't feel or see it, thank You for persistently loving me anyway. I rest knowing You are my Good Shepherd. Because of You, I never have been, nor will be, in want.

TABLE OF CONTENTS

FOREWORD

WHEN I BECAME A CHRIST-FOLLOWER in college, I recall hearing Billy Graham say that he read five psalms and one proverb every day—along with a portion of the Old Testament and New Testament. I heard that and thought, "If that's what Billy Graham does, then I want to do it, too."

By God's grace, for over twenty years, I have followed this plan in general, with special time devoted to reading and praying the Psalms in particular. I don't say this to boast but to confess. I don't read the Psalms because I'm a good Christian. I read and pray the Psalms because I'm a desperate man. I need God every day. I need to be reminded of His greatness, glory, mercy, and kindness. I need to be reminded that I'm not alone in my grief, despair, and discouragement. I need to be reminded to preach to my soul (like the Psalmist does in Psalm 42). I need to tremble at God's holiness. And I need to savor the Savior through the Psalter, for all of Scripture points to Him.

The Psalms are such a treasure to the believer. Every human emotion is touched. An early church father, Athanasius, quipped, "The Bible speaks to us, but the Psalms speak for us." Often, I don't have the words to pray, but I have the church's prayer and praise book in the Psalms; and it helps give voice to my thoughts, emotions, problems, and victories.

Jesus loved the Psalms. He died with the Psalms on His lips, and they appear throughout His teachings. Meditating and memorizing the Psalms follow the pattern of Jesus.

A handful of psalms speak to individual believers in powerful ways during particular seasons of life. At various points in my Christian journey, I have memorized certain psalms. One year, I memorized Psalm 119, which has 176 verses. It was an edifying endeavor. People ask me to recite it, and I say, "I hid it in my heart, and I don't know where I put it." But I can recite aspects of it, and it moves me as I think about God's Word. Psalm 103 has also been a psalm I have loved to cite. On many mornings, with coffee in hand, I walk outside and voice God's Word out loud. What a gift the Psalms are.

I could mention other famous psalms, such as Psalms 2 and 110, but any discussion of memorable and edifying psalms must include Psalm 23.

In Psalm 23, David speaks for us as we try to deal with despair and anxiety in life. All of us experience seasons of defeat and weariness, and in these times, we need to remember who the Lord is. He is our Shepherd, and He has everything we need. Our Shepherd feeds us with the green pastures of His Word.

Anxiety can overwhelm us. Our children may be struggling with temptations and trials. Perhaps a parent has been diagnosed with cancer. Maybe we are enduring the stress of work and providing for our family. David reminds us the Lord walks with us through the dark valley, that the Lord is the Restorer of our souls, and that the Lord leads and comforts us. Our Lord promises us that goodness and mercy will follow us all the days of our lives and that we will dwell with Him forever. And this shepherdly care points us ahead to Jesus, Who is revealed in the New Testament as our Good Shepherd (John 10:11), our Great Shepherd (Hebrews 13:20), and our Chief Shepherd (1 Peter 5:4).

All of these truths and more are presented in compelling and beautiful ways in Pastor Mark Becton's *Praying with David: Honest Prayers for Hard Seasons*. When Pastor Mark speaks to our students, everyone leans in. He has not only walked with God for a long time, but he has also walked with God for a long time through many hard seasons. I'm glad to see this book in print because more people can be blessed by Pastor Mark's ministry. Readers will see his skill in communicating. More importantly, they will be blessed by how his teaching overflows with genuine love for the Father. If you're interested in a wise, experienced saint who has experienced God in the highs and lows of life and who will speak to you in the highs and lows of your life, then journey with him in this book as he helps us consider the Lord's leadership, peace, restoration, guidance, comfort, graciousness, goodness, mercy, and presence.

TONY MERIDA, PHD
Pastor for Preaching and Vision, Imago Dei Church, Raleigh, NC
Dean of Grimké Seminary

PREFACE

AS A FELLOW READER, I know the process. If we connect with a book's title, we scan the table of contents. That means by now, you've seen the focus of this book is Psalm 23, which may raise some questions.

First, "Why write on Psalm 23?" Philip Keller's timeless classic, *A Shepherd Looks at Psalm 23*, is still accessible to readers. Furthermore, many are already familiar with this psalm and quote it effortlessly. What can be said about the psalm that hasn't already been said or thought?

Second, "What type of book is this?" Is it a devotional that prompts prayer or a deeper study? Is it like Keller's work—someone's journey through Psalm 23? Again, I'm a reader, too, and these would be my questions. Fortunately, I'm also the writer, so let me answer them.

This didn't begin as a book. It was a series of lessons that kept re-surfacing. Birthed as sermons, I was later asked to teach them as a seminar. Soon, I saw the truths kept popping up in conversations. And now, as I teach future pastors, I see how the honesty of David's life and prayers are crucial in helping pastors endure.

But again, why write it? Why not tell others to read Keller or pick up a good commentary? I could do that, and, in some ways, I do. I mention insights from Keller and other authors throughout.

Writing this book was for my benefit. God used it to grow me. There's nothing as memorable as working through something and discovering the sweet truths for ourselves. That's why it keeps appearing when talking with family, friends, fellow believers, and pastors.

There is, however, an overlooked benefit of another book on Psalm 23: perspective. None of us can ever surface all the priceless pearls from a passage. But surrounding ourselves with others who marvel over a text and who worship God with what He reveals deepens our understanding and awe.

It did that for me. Surrounding myself with other writers while cherishing the sweetness of the psalm, I stepped into their awe of God. I hope that by adding this book, it adds one more voice worshipping God and soon moves you to worship Him also.

The more practical question is "How should I read this book?" Should you read it as a devotional, Bible study, or the author's journey?

I'm afraid to say the answer is yes. I don't like this answer because if a book tries to become too many things, it becomes nothing valuable to the reader. However, those who read my early manuscript said they made it a part of their devotions. That every chapter encourages and guides in prayer makes it a good devotional read.

The chapters also provide depth for the believer who loves a rich study. You'll see the context behind Psalm 23 and other psalms David wrote. I love word studies. Going deeper into how a word is used in this psalm and other passages adds precision, emotion, and understanding.

Finally, the Father took me on a personal journey with this book. David's life became personal to me. I believe that was God's intent for preserving so many stories in Scripture. We step into them. See them. Feel them. Relate to them. In doing so, we see God's nature through them.

That's why David's psalms, his preserved prayers, describe God in ways that move us. It becomes personal, and it speaks to us on our journey as well.

Thus, how do you read this book? Read it as a devotional, Bible study, and a record of a personal journey. I'm asking the Father to reveal Himself to you as He did David and as He has to me. May you worship Him as you read.

CHAPTER ONE

WHY PRAY PSALM 23?
DEPENDENCE ON GOD!

The Lord is my shepherd;
I shall not want.
He makes me to lie down in green pastures;
He leads me beside the still waters.
He restores my soul;
He leads me in the paths of righteousness
For His name's sake.
Yea, though I walk through the valley of the shadow of death,
I will fear no evil;
For You are with me;
Your rod and Your staff, they comfort me.
You prepare a table before me in the presence of my enemies;
You anoint my head with oil;
My cup runs over.
Surely goodness and mercy shall follow me
All the days of my life;
And I will dwell in the house of the Lord
Forever.

—Psalm 23

I'VE QUOTED THIS COMFORTING LYRIC beside hospital beds and gravesides and shared it with stressed friends. As I get older, I yearn more for its soothing truths.

I surrendered to Jesus at six, started preaching at sixteen, and began pastoring at twenty. Yet today, it's emotionally harder to follow Jesus. It demands more determination to renew my mind, more discipline to pray, and more strain to obey. I thought it got easier with each birthday, but at times, it's harder.

I'm strangely comforted, however, in the discomfort of others. I remember reading about Martin Luther[1] and Charles Spurgeon's[2] battles with depression and missionary Adoniram Judson's dark night of the soul.[3] More recently, Mother Teresa's hidden anguish surfaced with the publication of her private writings.[4]

Seeing the hard seasons of others following Jesus, I realize we should expect our own. God purposes painful seasons to keep us dependent on Him. Through dependence, God keeps us close. And while dependent, we learn God's amazing attributes—those things that make Him our Good Shepherd.

PRAYING PSALM 23 ADDRESSES OUR TENSION

Depending on God taxes us. The *English Oxford Dictionary* explains why dependence is difficult. It first defines *dependent* as "contingent on or determined by."[5] We hear this every day when we say, "Well, it depends." We can't answer because of too many uncertainties. It's so frustrating, and we all feel it. How can we make decisions and set plans when it always depends on something beyond our control?

---

1   Roland Bainton, *Here I Stand: A Life of Martin Luther* (New York: Abingdon Press, 1950), 359-363.
2   Richard Ellsworth Day, *The Shadow of the Broad Brim: The Life Story of Charles Haddon Spurgeon Heir of the Puritans* (Philadelphia: The Judson Press, 1934), 171-179.
3   "Missionary Biographies: Adoniram Judson, A Baptist Page Portrait," 1997-2001, The Baptist Page online, http://www.wholesomewords.org/missions/bjudson20.html.
4   Shona Crabtree, "Book Uncovers a Lonely, Spiritually Desolate Mother Teresa," *Christianity Today* online, August 30, 2007, http://www.christianitytoday.com/ct/2007/augustweb-only/135-43.0.html.
5   *Oxford English Dictionary Synonyms, and Spanish to English Translator,* Oxford Lexico, s.v. "dependent," accessed May 1, 2022, https://en.oxforddictionaries.com/definition/dependent.

Being dependent is also defined as "requiring someone or something for financial or other support."[6] Tax forms reveal this when asking how many dependents we have.

Combining these definitions, we can see why faithfully following Jesus requires dependence and why dependence over time is so draining. We become God's dependent and depend on Him for everything every day.

If someone asks us about our plans for the rest of our week, year, or life, we can truthfully say, "It depends on God." He can change our circumstances, direction, and plans at any time. That's why being in control of our resources and plans actually feels easier, while depending on God for these leaves us tired and frustrated . . . until we see the benefit.

David shares the benefit of depending on God: over time it produces experiences with God and a knowledge of God that leaves us in awe of Him. Throughout his psalms, David calls God the following:

Elohe Chaseddi—"God of Mercy" (Psalm 59:10)

Elohei Tehillati—"God of My Praise" (Psalm 109:1)

El Hakabodh—"God of Glory" (Psalm 29:3)

Elohim Machase Lanu—"God Our Refuge" (Psalm 62:8)

Eli Maelekhi—"God My King" (Psalm 68:24)

El Nekamoth—"The God Who Avenges" (Psalm 18:47)

Elohim Ozer Li—"God My Help" (Psalm 54:4)

Elohim Shophtim Ba-arets—"The God Who Judges in the Earth" (Psalm 58:11)

Elhohe Tishuathi—"God of My Salvation" (Psalm 51:4)

Elohe Tsadeki—"God of My Righteousness" (Psalm 4:1)

Jehovah Gibbor Milchamah—"The Lord Mighty in Battle" (Psalm 24:8)

Jehovah El Emeth—"Lord God of Truth" (Psalm 31:5)

Jehovah Elohim Tsaba—"Lord God of Hosts" (Psalm 59:5)

Elohim Chasidi—"God of Loving Kindness" (Psalm 59:17)

---

6   Ibid.

Jehovah Mephalti—"The Lord My Deliverer" (Psalm 18:2)

Jehovah Metsudhathi—"The Lord My High Tower" (Psalm 18:2)

Jehovah Sali—"The Lord My Rock" (Psalm 18:2)

Jehovah Ori—"The Lord My Light" (Psalm 27:1)

Jehovah Uzzi—"The Lord My Strength" (Psalm 28:7)

Ab'—"Father" (Psalm 68:5)

Jehovah Rohi—"The Lord My Shepherd" (Psalm 23:1)[7] [8]

Psalm 23 rehearses what David learned about God from his seasons of dire dependence. For us, it produces a timeless and encouraging prayer. It not only encourages us to trust God with the unknowns but also surfaces an eagerness that seems out of place.

Praying Psalm 23, we face our moments of dependence and wonder what great experiences with God and amazing truths about God we will discover. Our tension from dependence on God is replaced by anticipation of experiences with God.

PRAYING PSALM 23 ADDRESSES OUR NEEDS

Our tension from depending on God comes from several pulls. David may have written Psalm 23 near the end of his life.[9] Those draining tugs influenced his thoughts when penning the psalm. Those same taxing tensions affect us. They include heavy responsibilities, wrong expectations, sinful consequences, and exhaustion.

HEAVY RESPONSIBILITY

In 1 Samuel 16, David feels Samuel's oil dripping from his head. God's revered prophet may have leaned in and said, "Young man, you are God's

---

7   Tony Evans, *Praying Through the Names of God* (Eugene, Oregon: Harvest House Publishers, 2014).

8   John Phillips, *Exploring the Psalms: Psalms 1-88* (Neptune, New Jersey: Loizeaux Brothers, 1988), 14. Phillips lists the Psalms ascribed to David. They include Psalm 3-9; 11-32; 34-41; 51-65; 68-70; 86; 101; 103; 108-110; 122; 124; 131; 133; 138-145.

9   Kyle M. Yates, *Studies in Psalms* (Nashville: Broadman Press, 1953), 35.

future king of Israel."[10] Around the age of a high school freshman, David had only known shepherding sheep. Yet for the rest of his life, he would carry the responsibility of leading Israel.

Many, like me, surrendered to Jesus as a child. Some mistakenly thought that was all God asked. In their mind, their baptism was one-and-done. They were saved from Hell. All they needed to do from then on was go to church and be good.

At some point, God makes us aware of our heavy responsibility to follow Jesus' lead in all things. We must follow wherever He leads and obey whatever He purposes. We must submit our will and resources to Him. We should honor Him through our role in our family, at work, and in relationships. We are to continue Jesus' mission in living, speaking, and spreading the Gospel to the ends of the earth.

Feeling the tension from our responsibility in following Jesus, we acknowledge it's impossible to do this without God's help. We depend on Him.

WRONG EXPECTATIONS

Fifteen years lapse between David feeling the oil and his wearing the crown.[11] During that time, he lives in caves with others as a fugitive from his father-in-law, King Saul, who wants him dead. As nomads, David and his supporters try to survive in enemy lands. David can easily lament, "Did I hear right? Wasn't I anointed to be king? Yet I'm not respected as one, nor do I have any of the perks of being king." Still, David is faithful to God and eventually becomes king. He relies on God, especially when confused by God's activity or inactivity.

As Christ-followers, we set ourselves up for difficulty. We expect—and sometimes are taught—that Jesus blesses and protects His followers. Therefore, we should experience promotions, not job loss; good health, not cancer; and a loving family, not a family at odds with each other and God.

---

10   F. B. Meyer, *Great Men of the Bible, Vol. 2* (Grand Rapids: Zondervan, 1982), 14.
11   Walter C. Kaiser Jr., Duane A. Garrett, *NIV Archaeological Study Bible* (Grand Rapids, Michigan: Zondervan, 2005), 395.

Like David, though, we are called to a purpose, not a bubble. David would serve God by serving the people as king and honor God with whatever God purposed. Remaining faithful in moments when our expectations of life and God are not the same as God's requires dependence. God knows what He's doing, even though it's not what we expected.

SINFUL CONSEQUENCES

Finally wearing his crown, David enjoys the benefits of his obedience. He builds a palace and sends generals to fight his battles. Feeling entitled as king, David has an affair with Bathsheba. When he learns she's pregnant, he arranges her husband's death. This allows David to marry her to hide his sin. But the rippling consequences of his sin divide his kingdom. David's son Absalom leads a coup to overthrow him. David narrowly escapes but once again is a fugitive.

There is a difference between David's two seasons as a fugitive. The first time, he did nothing wrong but, rather, suffered because of King Saul's jealousy. Although Absalom is not blameless, this time, the real blame is David's. Psalm 51 records David's prayer of repentance. Still, David needed to depend on God to help him weather the consequences of his sin.

God's forgiveness is merciful and complete, but we still must face sin's fallout. We must repair relationships, restore trust, regain health, change habits, address finances, and confront bitterness and grudges. Sometimes, sin's impact feels overwhelming. That's when, like David, we fall before God in prayer and rely on His strength and help.

WORN OUT

After a while, depending on God can wear on us—the burden of all He asks, the confusion over His activity, and the pain of trying to climb out from the consequences of our sins. We feel we have nothing left. Our prayer sounds like David's desperate plea in Psalm 142:1-3:

I cry out to the Lord with my voice;
With my voice to the Lord I make my supplication.
I pour out my complaint before Him;
I declare before Him my trouble.

When my spirit was overwhelmed within me,
Then You knew my path.
In the way in which I walk
They have secretly set a snare for me.

David prayed this prayer while hiding from Saul in the Cave of Adullam. Tired of being chased and weary from trying to stay godly and obedient, David was drained. Although Scripture does not record it, I wonder if David thought, *God, I'm done. I want to do what I want to do the way I want to do it whenever I want. Get someone else to be king. Let someone else depend on You.*

David prayed this before he was crowned king. Near the end of his forty-year reign (1010-970 B.C.), David penned Psalm 23. In it, he reflects on God's faithfulness to him long after he cried to God in the cave.

David didn't quit. He didn't walk away from what God asked or allowed. He didn't even walk away when he blew it with Bathsheba. He continued to depend on God because he kept praying, and his prayers were direct.

As a pastor, I've taught from passages because they addressed my need. Sometimes, I preached texts knowing they met the needs of others. This time, it's both.

We can all learn from David's life and prayers because we know how it feels to depend on God. David also shows us the beauties of God's nature—beauties we can only see when depending on Him. That's why God purposed David's experiences and preserved His prayers in Scripture. They not only lead us to stand in awe of God, but they also lead us to pray specifically.

PRAYING PSALM 23 IS SPECIFIC

Many are familiar with the Psalms, but few see them like Thomas G. Long. He calls them "poetic liturgical prayers."[12] H. C. Leupold says David took his poetic prayers and handed them to the choirmaster to be used in public worship.[13] Once used in worship, the people remembered them, and they became a part of their devotions and prayers.[14]

These psalms are still powerful devotional pieces because they are emotionally raw and genuine. John Calvin called the psalms "The Anatomy of all Parts of the Soul" and said they address "all the griefs, sorrows, fears, misgivings, hopes, cares, anxieties; in short, all the disquieting emotions with which the minds of men art wont to be agitated."[15]

Like the perfect Hallmark card, the Psalms seem to say what we feel and request of God what we want. That's the beauty of Psalm 23.

Because Psalm 23 is Hebrew poetry, rhyme is not present. However, like all poetry, every word is packed with imagery and meaning.[16] That's why each verse points to a moment of David's extreme dependence on God. They magnify attributes of God as seen through dependent eyes and also inspire us to pray.

A slow walk through Psalm 23 will help us to endure those seasons when we can't make it without depending on God.

PRAYING PSALM 23 WORKS

In the heart of the twentieth century, notable pastor and author Charles Allen frequently prescribed Psalm 23. To anyone stressed, hopeless, and drained, he wrote on a piece of paper, "Take Psalm 23 five times a day for seven days." Like a detailed prescription, he instructed them to read it slowly

---

12 Thomas G. Long, *Preaching and the Literary Forms of the Bible* (Philadelphia: Fortress Press, 1989), 44.
13 H. C. Leupold, *Exposition of the Psalms* (Columbus, Ohio: The Wartburg Press, 1959), 9.
14 Long, 44.
15 G. Campbell Morgan, *Notes on the Psalms* (Old Tappan, New Jersey: Fleming H. Revell, 1947), 6.
16 Long, 44-45.

and to meditate on each word and phrase when they woke up, ate each meal, and went to bed. They were not to stop after three days if they felt better. For the greatest benefit, they had to finish the prescription.

Allen explains why his prescription worked: "It contains 118 words. One could memorize it in a short time. Most of us already know it. But its power is not in memorizing its words, but rather in thinking the thoughts."[17]

I'm not prescribing Psalm 23 to re-orientate our thoughts but to re-shape our prayers. I did the same thing with the Lord's Prayer, and to this day, it remains a valuable tool to realign my life. By praying Psalm 23 slowly, it will do what it says midway: restore our souls. Only then can we pray and depend on God to the end—and along the way be amazed by His kindness and strength.

So, let's get started.

---

17   Charles L. Allen, *God's Psychiatry*, reprinted (New York: Jove/HBJ Books, 1978), 15.

CHAPTER TWO

BE MY SHEPHERD: I NEED A LOT!

"The Lord is my shepherd; I shall not want."

—Psalm 23:1

AS A YOUNG MAN, I listened to a sermon by S. M. Lockridge. I heard him say, "In sin, man declares his independence from God. But in prayer, he declares his dependence upon God." He was right.

As Jesus' followers, we live as God's dependents. Our directions, decisions, plans, and purpose depend on God's leading. Our resources to follow Him depend on His daily supply. Our strength to overcome and endure all of life's challenges depends on the assurance of His presence and promises. David understood this.

Psalm 23 represents David's poetic prayer. He writes at the end of his life as a dependent sheep praising God, his Shepherd. If we recall some of David's experiences, we can understand why he depended on God and why he praised Him in prayer. David's reasons are often ours.

In David's lifetime, he experienced:
- Being at odds with his boss, who happened to be his father-in-law (1 Samuel 18-26).
- Being mistreated for doing what was right (1 Samuel 18-26).
- Having to ask for food from a pastor (1 Samuel 21:1-6).
- Enduring the pain of divorce (1 Samuel 18:27; 25:43-44).
- Mourning the death of a dear friend (1 Samuel 18:1; 31:1-2).

- Being confused over God's will or timing (1 Samuel 16-2 Samuel 5).
- Blowing it with God and his family by having an affair (2 Samuel 11:1-12:15).
- Experiencing the death of a newborn (2 Samuel 12:15-22).
- Suffering hurt over rebellious children (2 Samuel 13:1-20; 15-18).
- Dealing with a daughter being raped (2 Samuel 13:1-20).
- Mourning an adult child murdered (2 Samuel 13:21-33).
- Losing his job and his home (2 Samuel 15:13-14).
- Having an adult child killed in war (2 Samuel 18:14-15).
- Seeing his life's dream given to another (1 Chronicles 28:1-10).
- Carrying great responsibility when all he probably wanted to do was tend sheep (1 Samuel 16).

We hope our season of dependence on God is short. We want to live it, learn from it, and then be released from it, never needing dependence again. Yet, the above list shows life stringing one dependent experience after another. Gratefully, David's psalm is an homage to God for proving faithful in all his experiences.

David's prayer highlights an important principle in living and praying dependently on God—we must constantly refocus our eyes on God. Jesus teaches this in His model prayer. It opens in Matthew 6:9, "Our Father in heaven, Hallowed be Your name." Before making any request of God, Jesus tells us to realize whom we are addressing.

David does something similar in his prayer. Human nature leads us to obsess over the size and nature of our problems. We counter that by looking away from them and focusing on God's size and nature—an effective practice I learned as a child.

I first got glasses in the fourth grade. Before sending me out, the optometrist shared an important lesson. He said, "When focusing on something up close for long periods of time, occasionally look up. Find a distant tree and focus on the leaves. Doing so rests your eyes. It also helps them focus better on what's up close."

Opening our prayer by focusing on God instead of our problems rests our eyes. It also resets them when looking back at previous problems. We see them differently, even creatively. Focusing on God's size, God's nature, our relationship with Him, and His history with us and others enables us to continue praying and depending on God.

FOCUS ON GOD'S SIZE

Martin Luther and Erasmus were pen "pests" not "pals." Exchanging letters in the sixteenth century, they held each other theologically accountable. One statement by Luther to Erasmus highlights a timeless trait in human nature. Luther told Erasmus, "Your thoughts of God are too human."[1]

Fear causes us to humanize God. Fearing the ripples of downsizing at work; the unknowns behind our doctor calling for a battery of tests; and the "what ifs" if we can't restore the relationship with our spouse, parents, or children leads to tunnel vision. The more we look at the problem, the larger it gets, and the smaller God becomes.

David did not have my optometrist, but he practiced his advice. David stopped, looked up and away from his fear, and reset his eyes. He focused on God's size when he addressed God as "the Lord." The Hebrew word is *Yahweh*. In Latin, it's *Jehovah*. The word is used more than sixty-five hundred times in the Old Testament and is packed with meaning.[2]

Surprisingly, this is not the first name given to God. God first introduces Himself as *Elohim* in Genesis 1:1. God repeats this thirty-four times before finally calling Himself *Yahweh* in Genesis 2:4. Yahweh means "I am," while Elohim means "strong One." God introduces Himself first as the strong One because He is.[3]

---

1   Arthur Pink, *The Attributes of God* (Grand Rapids, Michigan: Baker Book House, 1975), 28.
2   Tony Evans, *The Power of God's Names* (Eugen, Oregon: Harvest House Publishers, 2014), 42.
3   Ibid, 32.

As Elohim, God created:

- Time as we know it: "In the beginning God created the heavens and the earth" (Genesis 1:1).
- Something out of nothing: "The earth was without form and void" (Genesis 1:2).
- Light out of darkness: "Then God said, 'Let there be light,' and there was light" (Genesis 1:3).
- Order for life: "Then God said, 'Let the water under the heavens be gathered into one place, and let the dry land appear.' And it was so" (Genesis 1:9-13).
- Order with purpose: "Then God said, 'Let there be lights in the firmaments of the heavens to divide the day from the night; and let them be for signs and seasons and for days and years'" (Genesis 1:14).
- Order with beauty: "Then God said, 'Let the waters abound with an abundance of living creatures, and let birds fly above the earth across the face of the firmament of the heavens'" (Genesis 1:20).
- Us: "So God created man in His *own* image; in the image of God He created him; male and female He created them" (Genesis 1:27).[4]

Yet the word used most to describe God is Yahweh—I Am. God is personal. More than just a strong being, He is capable of and longs for us to know Him deeply. Seeing God that way dramatically resets our eyes.

As Yahweh, God is the relational one. Therefore:

- When overwhelmed, remember God purposes all things so that we know Him, His abilities, and His nature. Then, we can trust, worship, and follow Him.
- When stressed over waiting on God or anxious because He's moving too fast, remember we're praying to the One Who created and controls time. He can stop or stretch it when He wants.

---

4   Ibid, 25-40.

- When hopeless for a remedy, remember we pray to the One Who created everything out of nothing.
- When blind to a solution, remember we're asking the One Who created light out of darkness.
- When all around us seems chaotic and purposeless, remember we're petitioning the One Who gave order, purpose, and beauty to everything.
- When we or the doctors struggle for answers, remember we pray to the One Who created us. He knows what's wrong and what's needed.

Focusing solely on our problem over time distorts everything. Our thoughts of God become too human, making our problems too big and God too small. The practice of opening prayer by looking away from our problem and up to God resets our eyes, enabling us to see God and life appropriately—until God doesn't answer our prayer the way we expected.

As anger and bitterness seep in, we risk having our view of God become too human again. That's why we need a better appreciation of God as Yahweh.

FOCUS ON GOD'S NATURE

David starts his prayer with the verb *is*, which is important. Without it, we focus on God's size—all He can do—but not His nature—the reason for His actions. By adding the present tense of the verb, David reminds himself and us that God's abilities, thoughts, will, and nature are greater than ours. God's view and purpose are always greater than ours.[5]

But that's hard to accept when God does not answer our prayer and we carry pain. I learned that on my fifty-fifth birthday when I bought a bicycle and accompanied my son on a bike trail. It was great. We didn't have to worry about cars or pedestrians. It was just my bike and my son. Riding

---

5   Ibid, 44.

was a worship experience as we passed fields of corn, wheat, and peanuts. I thanked God for His creation.

Four miles into our ride, the factory seat on my cheap bike felt like marble. At mile six, I said, "Son, I need to head back. My backside's killing me." By mile eight, we had returned to the fields where I once worshipped. I tried worshiping again, hoping it would distract me from the pain. But the ride soon turned into a self-loathing exercise as I said to myself, "I can't believe I bought a bike at fifty-five. What was I thinking?"

That pain and struggle to worship God came to mind weeks later as I prayed with a friend. We had prayed for two years for his daughter, who was a mother of five with a debilitating disease. Although we prayed for God's healing and for God to give doctors His knowledge of what to do, she continued to decline. The doctors said, "There's nothing more we can do."

The next time we prayed, all I could say was "Father, I trust You, but I don't understand."

When I finished, my friend said, "Mark, that's all my wife and I can pray now. We know God does all things for His glory. We've seen our daughter glorify Him to her doctors and others through what He's allowed, but, still, it hurts."

To keep my thoughts of God from becoming too human—thinking God owes me; He's unfair; or He doesn't care—I often approach Him by listing His attributes. They trumpet His nature. In a sample prayer below, I highlight some of the names and attributes of God David uses, along with some I use.

God,

You are merciful, righteous, and strong.

You are the King Who judges in truth.

You are our Deliverer, Refuge, and Help.

You are holy, just, kind, and good.

You do what is right for Your glory.

When I see Your glory, my joy is full, and I rest in You.

I've learned from David to open prayer by focusing on God's size and nature. This keeps my thoughts of God and life from becoming too human when my problems seem bigger than God. Resetting our eyes on God at the start of prayer also shrinks our sense of entitlement and increases our awe of God. This happens when we realize the Lord is our Shepherd.

FOCUS ON OUR RELATIONSHIP

Entitlement threatens the health of every prayer. That's why Jesus opens His model prayer with "our Father" not "my Father" (Matthew 6:9). We can easily see ourselves as the only ones in the world in need.

Praying with the plural pronoun widens our eyes so we see other believers praying and also remember many don't know the Shepherd (John 10:14-17). Suddenly, our request for a car repair, good grade, or healthy doctor's visit doesn't seem as critical.

Still, nothing is wrong with using the personal pronoun, as long as we pray with awe, not entitlement. In John 17, Jesus prayed with awe on the night before His crucifixion. He mentions God's glory eight times as He prays for Himself (vv. 1–5), His remaining eleven (vv. 6–19), and those who will believe the gospel they spread (vv. 20–26). Focusing on the beauty and benefits of God's glory, keeps us from sounding entitled when we pray.

Entitled prayers can be hard to recognize because they carry subconscious expectations of God. Although we may not say it aloud, the subtext of our prayer is "God, because You are my Shepherd, You are supposed to . . ." To guard our hearts from this, especially when fear and anxiety consume us, we need to stop, breathe, and humbly approach God in awe and say, "God, I can't believe You are my Shepherd."

David immerses His prayer in awe of God. Other Old Testament passages also refer to God as Shepherd. However, in those, God is portrayed as shepherding His chosen people, Israel.[6] David may be the first to see God as a personal Shepherd.[7] That view comes from his background of tending sheep.[8] Although shepherds in David's day cared for large herds, they often gave their sheep names. Recognizing the shepherd calling their name, the sheep followed.[9]

God shepherded all of Israel, but David was in awe that the great I Am knew him personally. As Jesus' followers, we should let our awe be even greater than David's. What Jesus says in John 10:14-15, 27-30 is true:

> I am the good shepherd; and I know My *sheep* and am known by My own. As the Father knows Me, even so I know the Father; and I lay down My life for the sheep. My sheep hear My voice, and I know them, and they follow Me. And I give them eternal life, and they shall never perish; neither shall anyone snatch them out of My hand. My Father, who has given *them* to Me, is greater than all; and no one is able to snatch *them* out of My Father's hand. I and *My* Father are one.

David calls God *Yahweh*—I Am—and *Rohi*—Shepherd. In John 10:14, Jesus announces that He is the Good Shepherd; and in verse thirty, He emphasizes that He and the Father are one.[10]

God walked among us as Jesus. The One Who made us sacrificed Himself for us—and not because we were lovable. We crucified Him. The only One Who is good made it possible for us to have a relationship with Him.[11]

Pain and confusion cause us to see only our needs. Our driving prayer is often for God to rescue us when it should be for Him to display His glory. Opening our prayers by acknowledging God's size and nature reminds us of our privilege to have Jesus as our Shepherd. Therefore, we should pray:

---

6   Warren W. Wiersbe, *The Bible Exposition Commentary, Old Testament, Wisdom and Poetry, Job-Song of Solomon* (Colorado Springs: David C. Cook, 2004), 135.
7   H. C. Leupold, *Exposition of the Psalms* (Columbus: The Wartburg Press, 1959), 209.
8   John Stott, *Favorite Psalms* (Chicago: Moody Press, 1988), 32.
9   Wiersbe, 135.
10 Charles Haddon Spurgeon, *Psalms* (Grand Rapids: Kregel Publications, 1968), 109.
11 Ibid, 107.

Jesus, I know You and God are one (John 10:30). You created everything (John 1:1-5). I can't believe someone with Your abilities and nature would be my Shepherd.

Thank You for all You gave up in leaving Heaven for earth (Philippians 2:5-11). Thank You for all You endured and overcame while on earth—fatigue, hunger, thirst, pain, temptation. I can't believe Someone with Your abilities and nature would do all that to shepherd me.

My sin caused all Your pain. I'm still a chronic sinner today. Yet You saved me. You know my name. You call me and let me follow You. You remain with me, especially when following You is painful and confusing for me. You stay close even when I whine and complain.

Knowing all You are and have done and all I am and have done, I'm humbled You would be my Shepherd. Thank You, Jesus.

Praying this way refocuses us on what fulfills us the most: our awe of God in Jesus. But what comes next in David's prayer removes our panic when God doesn't seem to care for us the way we want.

FOCUS ON GOD'S HISTORY

David's last statement in verse one is our natural conclusion when considering God's size and nature and when believing that Jesus is our Shepherd. Regardless of what's before us, we can say with David that we will not want.

Hearing this as a child read in the King James Version, I overlooked two important truths. First, the Hebrew word for *want* means "to be in want." It doesn't mean God will fulfill our every desire but that we'll never have a need God will not meet. Furthermore, Jesus our Shepherd defines the need, not us.

As a child, although I circled everything in the Christmas catalog, I did not get everything I wanted. Still, I'm grateful Mom and Dad met my needs. But God does better. He discerns the difference between my wants and needs. Then, He meets my every need in a way that spotlights His glory.

Another often-overlooked truth lies in the grammar. David's statement is in the future tense.[12] Regardless of what comes, the Creator God—Whose nature is holy, right, and good—is with me. I say "I'm fine" with assurance to whatever comes.

But if I forget God is with me, if I find myself panicked over something too broken for me to fix or too big for me to overcome, I can reflect on my history with my Shepherd. David does this by calling God *Yahweh*. The name itself combines three tenses of the Hebrew word "to be." He's the One Who was, is, and always will be. That's why Jesus says of Himself in John 8:58, "Before Abraham was, I AM."[13] It's also why Hebrews 13:8 says of Jesus, He "is the same yesterday, today, and forever."

Because God cared for him in the past, David assures himself that God will also care for him in the present and future. Scripture is full of others like David whose accounts assure us of God's presence and care as our Shepherd.

But we have our own accounts of His care as well. In the sermon I heard from S. M. Lockridge, he also said, "Often, we spend more time numbering our bruises than counting our blessings. If we counted our blessings, it wouldn't be long, and we'd find ourselves on shouting ground with God." He was right again.

We should stop often and review our history with God—how He has protected, provided, and directed in our past. He's not weaker, nor has He forgotten our name. He is the same yesterday, today, and forever. Breathe. Regardless of what surfaces, the one who has shepherded us and others in the past is with us. The Creator of the universe Who is holy, righteous, and good is our Shepherd. Trust Him. Others will see the difference.

Decades ago, people who hosted parties invited their guests to sing or recite something. At one party, a famous actor was asked to recite Psalm 23.

---

12   H. C. Leupold, *Exposition of the Psalms* (Columbus, Ohio: The Wartburg Press, 1959), 210.
13   John Phillips, *Exploring the Psalms: Psalms 1-88* (Neptune, New Jersey: Loizeaux Brothers, 1988), 175.

Seeing an old and respected minister at the party, the actor said, "I'll recite it first if the minister will do so after me." The minister agreed.

As the actor recited the psalm, he used perfect pitch, tone, and inflection. When he finished, everyone applauded. As everyone quieted, the old minister took his turn reciting the psalm. He didn't have years of voice training like the actor, but when he finished, the people were moved to tears.

A man standing beside the actor asked, "What was the difference?"

Smiling, the actor said, "I knew the psalm, but he knows the Shepherd."

We can experience rest, strength, hope, guidance, comfort, peace, confidence, and encouragement when reading David's prayer, for it's a praise. He remembers God providing all these things in his past. Praying this prayer, David breathes when his present is hard or his future uncertain. His past with God renews his trust.

When we pray the same way—letting our past give us rest in a hard moment or uncertain future—people will see we know the Shepherd, not just the psalm.

CHAPTER THREE

MAKE ME LIE DOWN: I NEED REST!

"He makes me to lie down in green pastures."

—Psalm 23:2a

DEPENDING ON GOD IS NOT for wimps. Life is easier when we live by our own purposes, standards, goals, and schedules. Knowing we can do this frees us, but it is agonizing when we realize we don't have a say in any of them. It exhausts us when everything depends on God. I'm confident David felt the drain. I would love to ask David the following:

- You're barely old enough to shave. Do you think you can kill Goliath? He'd likely say, "It depends on God."
- You're a fugitive from King Saul. Do you think you can hide from the entire Israeli army? Again, he might say, "It depends on God."
- Saul is dead and Israel wants you as king. Do you believe you have what it takes to lead a nation? He might answer, "It depends on God."
- You've had an affair. Your family and nation are divided against you. Can you restore your relationships with God, your family, and the nation? With his head in his hands, he would probably say, "It depends on God."
- God says Solomon will succeed you as king. Yet another is pulling a power play for the throne. In your old age, do you have

enough left to obey God to the end? He offers from experience, "It depends on God."

I think David gives the same answer because he knows he does not have it in him to overcome or fulfill any of these. He has faced a lifetime of crushing demands and odds. He has depended on God every day. He has also learned the only way to survive the weight of daily dependence is to stop regularly for rest.

David understood this valuable routine for his sheep. That's why his request for God to make him lie down sounds like a plea. Since David writes this at the end of his life, he is probably reflecting on how God made him lie down and rest and how valuable it was.

Our nature, like David's, is to do the opposite. When God presents us with overwhelming odds, we tend to work longer hours, concentrate harder, and use every gift we have. After a while, we feel as though we're pedaling without a chain—putting forth effort but getting nowhere.

To endure constant dependence on God, we need to pray as David did. "God, get my attention. Stop my panicked efforts. Make me lie down. If I'm going to stay faithful to what You ask of me, I need to rest in You."

The above prayer is good, but we need to understand why God makes us lie down, how He does it, and what to do when He does.

WHY GOD MAKES US LIE DOWN

When sheep lie down in green pastures, they do so because they feel safe and are at peace in their relationships. Nothing annoys them. They feel fulfilled.

Philip Keller, a shepherd-turned-author, explains in his popular work, *A Shepherd Looks at Psalm 23*, the requirements for sheep to lie down. The sheep must feel freedom from fear. Sheep are defenseless, thus skittish about everything. They must be free from friction with other sheep. Even sheep have relationship problems. Also, sheep must be unbothered by insects and parasites. Nagging pests drive them crazy. Finally, they must be assured of food. They like to feel full and confident about their next meal.[1]

The shepherd also knows if he doesn't meet these needs and get the sheep to lie down, they won't be healthy. They need to stop in the heat of the day, lie down, and chew their cud (undigested food).

The challenge for David and other shepherds was their inability to explain this concept to the sheep. Trying to would have looked silly. I once tried to explain something to our family dog. My boys still laugh about it.

But David can explain our need to us. David used sheep to say, "You need to rest. If you don't, God will make you. God knows you need to stop and digest who He is and how good He's been to you. It's for your good."

Sheep won't stop until they are full and assured of their next meal. They also quickly follow the lead of other sheep.[2] If one presses on, the others will follow—what we call herd mentality. We worry and work tirelessly because we are never satisfied. Even when all our needs are met, if those around us keep working for the scholarship we need, the promotion we want, or the car we want to drive, we follow their lead. The reason God makes us lie down is to remind us our greatest needs have been met in Jesus. We need to stop striving and rest.

God knew this restless pursuit was embedded in human nature. That's why He modeled rest for us in Genesis 1. He also placed it in the heart of the Ten Commandments. God calls for Sabbath rest throughout the Old Testament.

God commanded His people in the Old Testament to regularly observe Sabbath—to stop and rest. But the rest they practiced in the Old Testament only becomes personal and lasting through Jesus in the New Testament. Colossians 2:16-17 explains, "So let no one judge you in food or in drink, or

---

1   Phillip Keller, *A Shepherd Looks at Psalm 23* (Minneapolis, Minnesota: World Wide Publications, 1970), 35-36.
2   Susan Schoenian, "Sheep 201: A Beginner's Guide to Raising Sheep." Sheep 201, April 19, 2021, http://www.sheep101.info/201/behavior.html.

regarding a festival or a new moon or sabbaths, which are a shadow of things to come, but the substance is of Christ."

As the Good Shepherd, Jesus laid down His life for the sheep. Paying the debt for our sin, He satisfied our greatest need—restoring our relationship with God. We no longer have to work at this. Jesus did it. We can rest in Him.

Regardless of what we think we must have or what the herd around us panics over, we need to stop, breathe, and realize our greatest need has been met by Jesus. We can be satisfied sheep who lie down in green pastures, resting in who we are and all we have in Jesus.

Stopping to rest is one thing. Mediating while resting is another. For sheep, it's called chewing the cud. Sheep eat a lot of grass, but to digest it well and get the best benefit from what they eat, they bring it up from their stomach and chew it again. The process sounds crude, yet as a grade-school boy watching sheep around my grandparents' house, it entertained me.

As Jesus' followers, our understanding of all He did to meet our greatest need should keep growing. We cannot work for God's favor. Our identity as heirs with Jesus is set with God now and for eternity. But life has a way of making us feel unfulfilled and dissatisfied. That's why we need to be still and digest all we are and have in Jesus.

Meditating through prayer is not sitting cross-legged and humming.[3] Biblical meditation takes mental and spiritual work.[4] Joshua 1 and Psalm 1 both instruct us to meditate on God's Word day and night. Psalm 119, which is all about God's Word, tells us to mediate all day on God's ways, decrees, wonders, precepts, statutes, promises, and works (119:15, 23, 27, 48, 78, 97, 99, 148).[5]

When we meditate on these things, God reminds us of Who He is, how He works, and what His promises are. This perspective helps us discern the

---

3   James Strong, *New Exhaustive Strong's Numbers and Concordance with Expanded Greek-Hebrew Dictionary*. (Nashville, Tennessee; Thomas Nelson, 2003), np, Biblesoft PC Study Bible One Touch Professional Series.

4   David McCasland, compiler and editor, *The Quotable Oswald Chambers* (Grand Rapids, Michigan: Discovery House, 2008), 162.

5   David Platt, "Meditating on God's Presence," radical.net, 1:00:22, June 29, 2014, https://radical.net/message/meditating-on-gods-presence/.

truth about what's before us. This, in turn, shapes our response to whatever we are facing.

By lying down in green pastures, we process what God has said in His Word, what His view is of our circumstances, and how He'd have us respond. When I have a lot to process in prayer, I write my prayers to God.

God also makes us lie down to help us appreciate Jesus, our Shepherd. David knew it took a lot of work to make his sheep lie down. Fields had to be cleared. The sheep had no clue where the fields were, so he had to lead them there. He had to satisfy all their fears, keep them from being ugly to each other, remove any annoying pests, and fill their stomachs with food. And he had to do this consistently for them to trust and follow him. I wonder if, as a boy tending sheep, he ever wondered, "Do they even appreciate all I do for them?"

Being still with God and digesting all He is, has said, and is doing shapes our appreciation of Him. It did for David. Psalms 120-134 are called Psalms of Ascent. People prayed them and possibly sang them as they journeyed the hill country toward Jerusalem. Doing so prepared them to worship God when they arrived. David wrote four of those psalms: 122, 124, 131, 133. Throughout David's life, his still moments with God generated awe of God.

Our still moments should do even more as we process all Jesus has done for us as our Good Shepherd. He took our identity as sinners before God (2 Corinthians 5:21). Enduring God's wrath, He satisfied our debt to God (Romans 6:23). He drew us by His Spirit to repent and believe (John 6:40, 44; 16:8-11; Philippians 1:29). He then fills and covers us with Himself (John 14:15-18; 2 Corinthians 5:16-17). He gave us His righteous identity before God and opened our access to God and His resources by making us joint-heirs with Him (Romans 8:12-17).

We often live overwhelmed by life because we live underwhelmed over who we are, who our Shepherd is, and what He did and continues to do for us. We'd be healthier sheep if we prayed regularly. That's why God makes us lie down, even when we don't want to.

HOW GOD MAKES US LIE DOWN

Like most moms, my wife, Loree, made our boys nap. Our younger son, Lee, was a good nap-taker. Without argument, he climbed onto his bed and was soon out. Our older son, John Mark, didn't like naps. Even as a four-year-old, he presented his case to Loree: "I don't like naps. They give me a headache." Twenty-one years later, he passed the Virginia bar, but we knew at four he was a little lawyer.

Even lawyers submit to the judge. As the judge, Loree heard his case but ruled against him. He didn't have to go to sleep, but he did have to lie down and rest—sometimes because my Loree needed a break.

Most of us, like John Mark, don't want to stop. Although we benefit from the rest of digesting Jesus, we're overwhelmed by what's before us. Consumed by it, we make the most of every minute—trying to get it done or, at least, to get ahead.

We're stubborn. Like my son, we can plead our case to God and tell Him why we don't have time to be still in prayer, but eventually, He will make us lie down. If not by force, He will use our innate need for it. If neither of these work, He'll use circumstances to force it.

David points to the Shepherd's leading us beside still waters. When it comes to being still with God in prayer, Jesus leads by example.

J. Oswald Sanders highlights this. His writings and influence encouraged followers in the mid-twentieth century. The New Zealander's passion for the nations moved him as he led the China Inland Mission. Yet he knew it was too much for him. He could not faithfully follow Jesus without regular periods of stillness, and Jesus' example moved him to take them. Sanders writes:

> Christ spent full nights in prayer (Luke 6:12). He often rose before dawn to have unbroken communion with His Father (Mark 1:35). The great crises of His life and ministry began with periods of special prayer, as in Luke 5:16: "Jesus often withdrew to lonely

places and prayed"—a statement that indicates a regular habit. By word and example, He instructed His disciples on the importance of solitude in prayer. (Mark 6:46, following the feeding of the five thousand; Luke 9:28, preceding the Transfiguration).[6]

If Jesus modeled His need to be still with God in prayer, what makes us think we don't desperately need it. God knows we do and uses Jesus' example to encourage it.

Consider the experience David describes and Keller explains. We're a sheep lying down in a green pasture. That's not our nature. This means we feel safe. We are also at peace in all our relationships. That doesn't mean everyone loves us. It simply means we're not bothered by any relationships. Furthermore, nothing will pester or nag at us. In short, everything is good with us, others, and God. It's the sweetest fulfillment we've ever experienced.

Once we have tasted that, we know when we are missing it. When we miss it over time, our whole being longs to experience it again. We hear this in the opening to David's prayer in Psalm 63:1-2. He prays, "O God, You *are* my God; Early will I seek You; My soul thirsts for You; My flesh longs for You In a dry and thirsty land Where there is no water. So I have looked for You in the sanctuary, To see Your power and Your glory."

David's entire being "fainted" for God.[7] This is the only time this Hebrew word appears in the Old Testament.[8] Yet every God-follower can relate. Former experiences of resting in Jesus make us long to experience them again. As the longing grows, so will our intentionality to be still, rest, digest, and appreciate all Jesus is.

David was in Judah's wilderness when he wrote Psalm 63. He bolted from Jerusalem as his son Absalom tried to depose him. A series of sins in David's

6   J. Oswald Sanders, *Spiritual Leadership: Principles of Excellence for Every Believer*, second revision (Chicago: Moody Press, 1994), 87.
7   Robert G. Bratcher and William D. Reyburn, *UBS Old Testament Handbook Series: The Book of Psalm.* (United Bible Societies, 1978-2004), np, Biblesoft PC Study Bible One Touch Professional Series.
8   Wiersbe, 206.

life led to this. Aching for the times when all was good with God, he prayed, "I faint for those still times when I rested in You" (paraphrased).[9]

Charles Allen says from experience, "Sometimes God puts us on our backs in order to give us a chance to look up: 'He maketh me to lie down.'"[10]

Allen prescribed Psalm 23 to many, yet in the hospital himself, he confessed, "I was very unhappy. I had no time to be wasting there in bed. My calendar was full of good activities and the doctor had told me to cancel all my appointments for at least a month. A dear minister friend of mine came to see me. He sat down and very firmly said, 'Charles, I have only one thing to say to you—*He maketh me to lie down.*'"[11]

As our good Shepherd, Jesus leads intentionally.[12] He knows when we need to lie down, digest His Word, and focus on Him. He'll make those moments happen; and when He does, we need to ask, "What do we do once we get still in prayer?"

WHAT TO DO WHEN LYING DOWN

Whether begrudgingly or longingly, we've stopped. God has our attention, but how do we make the most of the time?

Our human nature makes us want to leverage God to do what we want and fix our problems. We can seek Him in prayer so He will remove our pain. If that's the aim of being still, we will miss the benefit.

In Acts 7, God did not deliver Stephen from the mob of angry Jews holding stones. Yet Stephen endured that fatally painful moment more at peace than those hurling stones. Without question, he had been with God.

Shadrach, Meshach, and Abednego had a godless king and nation oppose them. They were ordered to bow to an idol or be burned. Feeling the heat

9   Ibid.
10   Charles L. Allen, *God's Psychiatry* (New York: Jove/HBJ, 1978), 19.
11   Ibid, 18.
12   G. Campbell Morgan, *Great Chapters of the Bible* (Old Tappan: Fleming H. Revell Company, 1935), 57.

of the nearby furnace, they refused with confident resolve (Daniel 3). Their strength came because they had been with God.

God doesn't make us lie down in green pastures to reward us by removing our pain but to remind us of Who is with us—our Shepherd. Spending time with Jesus is the benefit.

REST, DIGEST, AND APPRECIATE

To get the greatest benefit of our time with Jesus, we must lie down, chew our cud, and appreciate Him. More specifically, we need to get alone and digest what's before us. One tool that helps me do this is a journal.

As I shared in *Prayer Works: When You Work at Prayer*, I agree with Carol Gelderman. She said, "Writing is the most exact form of thinking."[13] We can be so consumed with the complex problem before us we miss seeing the size of the Shepherd beside us. We can write out our prayers, making sure to include all aspects of our problem and how we feel about it. Then, we can describe our history with Jesus and list what we've seen Him do in the past. We can also talk about His attributes as portrayed in Scripture.

Before concluding our prayer, we should praise Jesus for being all-knowing. He knows better than us all that's before us. We can thank Him for not being distant, disinterested, or distracted. He's the Good Shepherd, Who is with us and cares. He will act on our behalf for His glory and benefit. That's a good thing because when He does, it leaves us more in awe of Him. And once in awe of Him, we rest.

If we wonder if writing our prayers helps, we should consider David. He wrote seventy-three of the 150 psalms. They are his written prayers. Reading them, we see him digesting the moment before him and experiencing the Shepherd beside him. In almost every psalm—even when he is running from Saul, has blown it with Bathsheba, or faces a rebellious son—David praises God.

---

13   Mark Becton, *Prayer Works When You Work at Prayer: Following Jesus' Example in Prayer* (Forest, Virginia: Publishers Solution, 2017), 115.

STAY UNTIL GOD IS FINISHED

Finally, we should remain still and lie down until God is finished with us. I remember Henry Blackaby, the author of *Experiencing God*, being asked, "I know you get up each morning at 4 a.m. to pray. How long do you pray?" Blackaby answered, "Till God is finished with me."

Most green pasture moments won't take as long if we have them frequently. They can take a while if we haven't or if our time with God has included more dictating than listening so we can digest what we need.

This happened to me one Saturday. As I was still with Jesus in prayer, He brought to mind sins in my life I had ignored. Knowing I needed to digest all He was doing, I reached for a legal pad and began writing. After filling a page, I asked if He was finished. He said no and revealed more. After two hours and three pages of sins, God finished.

I found Loree and read them to her—not only for accountability but also to share my intimate and amazing time with Jesus. I called other pastors and shared the experience with them. Like a sixteen-year-old who had just received a new car for his birthday, I was too amazed to keep the experience to myself. I had been with Jesus, and He had performed a deep work in me.

Ask Jesus to make you lie down in green pastures with Him. Plead with Him to help you digest all that He is, has done, and promised—along with all that is before you. When you are truly still with Jesus, stay down until the Good Shepherd is finished with you. You will not have wasted your time.

CHAPTER FOUR

LEAD ME TO STILL WATERS: I NEED STRENGTH!

"He leads me beside the still waters."

—Psalm 23:2

WITH MORE THAN FORTY YEARS of ministry experience, Dad warned me about depression. He said, "Son, remember. Unmet expectations, over time, lead to depression. Even those close to God can experience it." Reading the prayers of the giants of scripture, I have discovered Dad was right.

Moses expected to experience the Promised Land sooner than he did. Weary with Israel's constant whining and complaining, Moses told God, "I am not able to bear all these people alone, because the burden *is* too heavy for me. If You treat me like this, please kill me here and now—if I have found favor in Your sight—and do not let me see my wretchedness" (Numbers 11:14-15).

Elijah, the man God used to spark a national revival, felt it, too. Not all are happy with Israel's revival. Queen Jezebel threatened to kill Elijah. Running for his life, Elijah flopped under the shade of a broom tree and barked at God: "It is enough! Now, Lord, take my life, for I *am* no better than my fathers" (1 Kings 19:4b).

Jonah said it as well. Angry for all God had put him through—although it was his fault—he was furious that God spared Israel's enemy, the Ninevites. He erupted at God, "It is right for me to be angry, even to death" (Jonah 4:9).

All three had different expectations. Moses expected to quickly reach the Promised Land as a celebrated leader. Elijah anticipated all of Israel, including the king and queen, would love and thank him for what he did. Jonah wanted God to wipe out Nineveh because of their cruelty to Israel, not spare and bless them.

Over time, unmet expectations left each drained and depressed. They would have rather been dead than follow God's lead—for their lives to be over rather than to continue depending on God. David experienced it, too.

Because God inspired David to pen his prayers, David wrote about his internal struggles more than any others. His spiritual and emotional swings fill the psalms. But his prayer in Psalm 23 differs. He wrote it with a hand weathered from experiences with God; and his tone is not bitter, angry, or fearful. It's thankful because he had learned to adjust his expectations with prayer.

David's prayer that God led him beside still waters reveals a shift in expectations. It provides a realistic view of the Shepherd—He leads. It also offers an accurate view of us and our needs: we are dependent, and we need still waters.

Once we retain a more realistic picture of ourselves, Jesus, and life, our prayers become more trusting, patient, purposeful, and thankful. We persevere more than threaten to quit because we correct our view of ourselves and Jesus.

OUR NATURE

David is not the only one who sees us like sheep. The prophet Isaiah did (Isaiah 53:6), and so did Jesus (John 10:25-31). Like sheep, we are quickly sapped and will seek anything to revive us. We also easily panic and focus on the emergency at hand rather than the big picture. Seeing how our nature affects our life with God and our prayers humbles us.

Still water revives the sheep. Sheep are composed of seventy percent water.[1] Humans hold fifty to seventy-five percent water.[2] We, like sheep, know

---

1   Phillip Keller, *A Shepherd Looks at Psalm 23* (Minneapolis: World Wide Publications, 1970), 49-50.
2   Anne Marie Helmenstine, "How Much of Your Body Is Water?" ThoughtCo., updated March 29, 2017, https://www.thoughtco.com/how-much-of-your-body-is-water-609406.

how it feels to be dehydrated and then re-hydrated. More than refreshing, it's physically and emotionally revitalizing. Our whole outlook on life changes from desperate to happy and secure.

David writes of his moments of extreme spiritual dehydration. He tells God in Psalm 22:15, "My strength is dried up." In Psalm 32:4, he says, "My vitality was turned into the drought of summer." David also cries to God in Psalm 38:10, "My heart pants, my strength fails me."

David's situation highlights our constant need for spiritual re-hydration. That's why David uses the plural for water. The text literally says, "Beside waters of resting places."[3] Because of the constant exertion in following Jesus, we always need still waters—times of prayer when we are revived by our stillness with Jesus.

Like Moses, Elijah, and Jonah, great theologians, missionaries, and pastors have confessed their constant drain and need for prayer. Chuck Swindoll writes:

> Dietrich Bonhoeffer, for example, once admitted that his prayer experience was something to be ashamed of . . . E. M. Bounds Alexander Maclaren, Samuel Rutherford, Hudson Taylor, John Henry Jowett, G. Campbell Morgan, Joseph Parker, Charles Hadden Spurgeon, F. B. Meyer, A. W. Tozer, H. A. Ironside, V. Raymond Edman, William Culbertson, and on and on. Great men, strong Christian examples, magnificent models, yet you can hardly find one of that number who was satisfied with his prayer life.[4]

That means they wrote, preached, studied, and were sent by God more sapped than fulfilled. They, like us, were emotionally, mentally, and spiritually depleted by what Jesus asked. We become our own worst enemy when we drink from anything other than Jesus to satisfy our thirst.

When Isaiah describes us as sheep, He says we all have turned to our own way but that God has punished Jesus for our sins (Isaiah 53:6). By nature, we look to satisfy our desires our way, not God's. This leads to dehydration and desperation.

---

3   H. C. Leupold, *Exposition of the Psalms* (Columbus: The Wartburg Press, 1959), 211.
4   Charles Swindoll, *Strengthening Your Grip* (Waco: Word Books, 1982), 149.

According to Phillip Keller, thirsty sheep become restless sheep. To satisfy their thirst, they will look for anything to drink. Without the shepherd's direction, they'll drink water filled with parasites and other disease-causing germs.[5]

We do the same spiritually. Desperate to satisfy any depletion of life, we turn to quick fixes like pornography for the rush, food for its comfort, exercise for releasing endorphins, spending for the excitement, accomplishments for the satisfaction, and council of others for affirmation. Although such things can provide a quick fix, their quenching effect is short-lived. Each becomes a harmful spiritual parasite weakening us even more.

As a former shepherd, David knew sheep panicked easily. They veered from flowing water for good reason. Soaked wool sinks.[6] That's why shepherds knew where natural indentions collected rain. A Jewish guide pointed one out to our group while I was in Israel. He said it would have been a place for the still water about which David wrote.

Sheep panicked over the condition of the water—if it flowed or not. They also grew restless over their immediate need for it.[7] Thirsty with no water in sight, regardless of the shepherd's history of getting them to water, they panicked.

Like sheep, we panic when spiritually and emotionally drained. I pastored a church in western Oklahoma during an extended drought. Many were distraught over our lack of rain, so we prayed. Before praying, I asked a deacon, who operated a large farm, about his thoughts. Calmly, he said, "I'm not worried. I've never seen a drought the Lord didn't end with a good rain."

Others whose livelihood did not rely on rain panicked more than the farmer. The difference? He saw the long view with God. He had seen God end droughts in the past. He knew this drought would end, and another would take its place. He believed his Shepherd would lead him through it.

5   Keller, 50.
6   Charles L. Allen, *God's Psychiatry* (New York: Jove/HBJ, 1978), 20.
7   Keller, 50.

Before becoming drained, we need to see the big picture. Spiritual and emotional dehydration is a part of following Jesus. Though David didn't pen Psalm 84:5, he would have agreed with it. "Blessed *is* the man whose strength *is* in You, Whose heart *is* set on pilgrimage." Weakness comes and goes in our pilgrimage with Jesus, but we can trust His history with us. He strengthened us before and will do so again. And a benefit comes with being sapped—we thirst for Jesus.

JESUS' NATURE

We thirst for Jesus because His nature provides what we need to overcome what's draining us. Only in Jesus do we have an all-knowing Shepherd Whom we can trust as our Source of strength.

In Psalm 23:2, David describes God's leadership as both forceful and caring.[8] On one hand, He can make us lie down with circumstances that force it. On the other hand, His forcing hand becomes a caring one when He leads us beside still waters. The Hebrew word translated "leads" means "to lead gently."[9] He addresses our drain as a caring, all-knowing Shepherd.

Jesus later classified Himself as the Good Shepherd Who knows His sheep and is known by His sheep (John 10:14). Just as Eastern shepherds in Jesus' day named their sheep, so Jesus knows our names. As they could tell when their sheep were stressed and in need of water, so Jesus knows us better than we do. He knows when we are spiritually sapped and need strength. And He knows where we can find it. Jesus is our Still Waters.

Our sheep-like nature spiritually depletes us. David experienced it often. David identifies God as his Source of strength—his Still Waters.

- "I will love You, O Lord, my strength . . . *It is* God who arms me with strength, And makes my way perfect" (Psalm 18:1, 32).
- "The king shall have joy in Your strength, O Lord; And in Your salvation how greatly shall he rejoice" (Psalm 21:1).

---

8   Morgan, 57.
9   Wiersbe, 136.

- "The Lord *is* my strength and my shield; My heart trusted in Him, and I am helped" (Psalm 28:7a).
- "The Lord will give strength to His people; The Lord will bless His people with peace" (Psalm 29:11).
- "I will wait for You, O You his Strength; For God *is* my defense" (Psalm 59:9).
- "Seek the Lord and His strength; Seek His face evermore" (Psalm 105:4).

David learns from experience that his Shepherd and reviving Still Waters are the same. To strengthen us, God does not lead us to a place but to Himself. Jesus, as our Good Shepherd, says to come to Him when we thirst for righteousness (Matthew 5:6). He tells a woman at a well that He is the living water (John 4:14). Jesus invites those at a festival to come to Him and drink (John 7:37).[10]

Prayer keeps us from constantly feeling spiritually dehydrated and leads us to still waters—to Jesus.

PRAYING TO JESUS FOR STRENGTH

Surviving on droplets of dew, sheep can go for months without a good drink of still water; but they are only surviving, not thriving.[11] They are not moving, thinking, or reacting at full strength. This is another way we are like sheep.

We survive on spiritual droplets of dew when we could have deep, satisfying drinks of Jesus. Sometimes, we must experience complete spiritual dehydration for us to stop and drink in Him. That's where we find David in Psalms 57 and 142—in a cave, spiritually sapped and struggling. In his book, *David: A Man of Passion & Destiny,* Chuck Swindoll describes David's condition:

> David had bottomed out. In a downward swirl of events, he lost his job, his wife, his home, his counselor, his closest friend, and

10   Keller, 50-51.
11   Ibid.

finally, his self-respect. When we left him last, he was dribbling saliva down his beard and scratching the gate of the enemy like a madman. Realizing that his identity was known by the Philistines, he feigned insanity and then slipped out of the city of Gath. Once more he was a man on the run. So David departed from there to the cave of Adullam—1 Samuel 22:1.[12]

By absorbing David's two Cave of Adullam psalms, we learn how to pray when our nature thirsts for Jesus. We learn how to pray when we are spiritually "bottomed out."

David may have written Psalm 142 before others joined him in the cave.[13] He had nowhere else to go. Nothing was more pressing than this desperate moment when he was alone with God.

Jesus also practiced being alone with God. He teaches us to go into our private room and shut the door when we pray (Matthew 6:6). The King James Version translates "private room" as "closet." That's a great picture.

When guests come to our house, I doubt we say, "Look in all my closets. Step into the coat closet with me." Jesus used a word for "private room" or "closet," intending it to be somewhere we would be alone with Him.

When we pray, it should be an uninterruptable time. When we have young children, such time is more difficult to find—but not impossible. Also, we should make it an electronic-free zone. No television, cellphone, laptop, or tablet. We need this time with Jesus, and others need us to have it. Jesus deserves us at our best.

Another lesson from David concerns honesty. The heading of Psalm 142 is "A Davidic Maskil. When he was in the cave. A prayer." A Maskil is Hebrew for "instruction."[14] This prayer not only records David's effort to be strengthened by God, but it also instructs us how to pray to be strengthened by God.[15]

12   Charles R. Swindoll, *David: A Man of Passion & Destiny* (Dallas: Word Publishing, 1997), 71.
13   John Phillips, *Exploring the Psalms: Psalms 89–150* (Neptune: Loizeaux Brothers, 1988), 621.
14   Ibid
15   Charles Haddon Spurgeon, *Psalms*, David Otis Fuller, ed. (Grand Rapids: Kregel Publications, 1968).

Reading Psalm 142, we notice David's unfiltered honesty.

I cry out to the Lord with my voice;
With my voice to the Lord I make my supplication.
I pour out my complaint before Him;
I declare before Him my trouble.

When my spirit was overwhelmed within me,
Then You knew my path.
In the way in which I walk
They have secretly set a snare for me.
Look on my right hand and see,
For there is no one who acknowledges me;
Refuge has failed me;
No one cares for my soul.

I cried out to You, O Lord:
I said, "You are my refuge,
My portion in the land of the living.
Attend to my cry,
For I am brought very low;
Deliver me from my persecutors,
For they are stronger than I.
Bring my soul out of prison,
That I may praise Your name;
The righteous shall surround me,
For You shall deal bountifully with me."

David is in trouble and feels weak, boxed in without options, and alone. He is also honest about what he needs from God: mercy, rescue, and safety. Above all, he needs strength.

David journals a prayer in Psalm 142. When we journal prayer as David did, everything is placed before us. We write out what is happening around us, how we feel about it, and what we believe we need from God. This exercise prepares us for the next phase: praying for strength to submit to God's purpose.

Psalm 142 is not the only prayer David pens in the cave. He also prays Psalm 57. But instead of calling it a Maskil, David labels it as a Miktam, which means "mystery poem." David addresses the mystery of how to experience strength when everything around us is draining everything from us. He answers the question in verses one and two:

> *Be merciful to me, O God, be merciful to me!*
> *For my soul trusts in You;*
> *And in the shadow of Your wings I will make my refuge,*
> *Until* these *calamities have passed by.*

> *I will cry out to God Most High,*
> *To God who performs* all things *for me.*

By combining David's prayers in Psalms 142 and 57, we find that prayer helps us define reality. Leadership author Max DePree says the primary job of any leader is defining reality for the organization.[16] The same is true in prayer.

Prayer allows us to process what's happening in our lives, how we feel about it, and what Jesus' nature is like. Doing this sets us up for a defining moment: determining God's purpose for us.

God's supreme purpose in all things and for everyone is to reveal His glory or greatness. Regardless of what He allows—prejudice from others, terminal

---

16   Max DePree, *Leadership Is an Art* (New York: Dell Publishing, 1989), 11.

cancer in a child, robbery, scamming, false accusations, unemployment—or what Jesus asks of us—to change careers, adopt a child, break off an engagement, address an injustice, have a spiritual conversation with a difficult person—we want to glorify God in it.

None of us enjoys the pain of abuse, the agony of confusion, or the frustration of change. Yet spending time with Jesus, knowing He does everything for His glory, gives us strength in a taxing moment. We experience the strength to honor Him with what He purposes. We experience such reviving strength that although the circumstances have not changed, we find ourselves praising Jesus amid them.

David concludes his prayer in the cave by praising God (Psalm 57:7-11). Reading it encourages me and makes me envious.

My heart is steadfast, O God, my heart is steadfast;
I will sing and give praise.
Awake, my glory!
Awake, lute and harp!
I will awaken the dawn.

I will praise You, O Lord, among the peoples;
I will sing to You among the nations.
For Your mercy reaches unto the heavens,
And Your truth unto the clouds.

Be exalted, O God, above the heavens;
Let Your glory be above all the earth.

Little had changed from what initially had caused David to spiritually hit bottom. Saul still wanted him dead, as did the Philistines. He was still in a cave and had no home, wife, job, counselor, close friend, or self-respect. Yet he praised God.

I envy David's sincere, unrestricted praise of God despite all he's going through. He has the peace, joy, trust, lightness, and strength for which I long. And yet, I'm encouraged. If David can experience such praise when sapped, so can all of us.

But which came first? Did a renewal of David's strength lead to his praise, or did his praise and trust in God despite his circumstance renew his strength? Does it matter? We can praise God before our strength is renewed. He is worthy, and Jesus is our Strength. He is with us whether we feel it or not.[17] If we don't, we may claim His strength as our own and take credit for our renewal when it was His doing all along.

THE STILL WATER EFFECT

Oswald Chambers made me think when I read, "The only way to know the strength of God is to take the yoke of Jesus upon us and learn of Him."[18] Let's put that in the context of everything we've learned about Jesus as our strength and still waters.

- The only way to know Jesus' strength and that He's with us is to engage in something beyond our strength. As we follow Jesus, we will always be engaged in such experiences. Acknowledging we are weak and dependent like sheep is a gift.
- Acknowledging our weakness makes us look to Jesus. We need to be still with Him and trust His strength.

---

17   We find David praising God in other psalms for the strength He gives. In Psalm 21:13, David writes, "Be exalted, Lord, in Your strength; we will sing and praise Your might." Also, in Psalm 28:7, David offers, "The Lord is my strength and my shield; my heart trusts in Him, and I am helped. Therefore my heart rejoices, and I praise Him with my song." And in Psalm 59:16–17, David extols, "But I will sing of Your strength and will joyfully proclaim Your faithful love in the morning. For You have been a stronghold for me, a refuge in my day of trouble. To You, my strength, I sing praises, because God is my stronghold—my faithful God."

18   David McCasland, complier and editor, *The Quotable Oswald Chambers* (Grand Rapids: Discovery House Publishers, 2008), 273.

- Trusting Jesus' strength enables us to continue our pilgrimage with Him and see Him do things we could never do without Him—things that point to His greatness, not ours, and things that leave us in awe of Him that erupts in worship and praise.

- Once we retain a more realistic picture of ourselves, Jesus, and life, our prayers become more trusting, patient, purposeful, and thankful. We persevere more than threaten to quit, all because Jesus corrected our view of ourselves and Him in prayer. By doing so, we regain our strength to depend on Him.

Regardless of what we face or how weary we feel, we can thank Jesus for being our Still Waters and renewing our strength in the draining experiences.

CHAPTER FIVE

RESTORE MY SOUL: I NEED HOPE!

"He restores my soul."

—Psalm 23:3a

WITH THE GREAT I AM as our Shepherd, Jesus meets every need, even though sometimes He must make us lie down to see it. But in the end, Jesus repeatedly satisfies our greatest need by restoring our souls.

Why does it seem our soul frequently needs restoring? Resting in Jesus—lying down in green pastures—realigns our eyes. Our view of all Jesus is and His true purpose for us gives us an assuring breath. Stopping to drink of Jesus—our Still Waters—revives us. But if we only take in droplets of Jesus instead of a full drink, we'll become desperate. Weeks or months of unaddressed desperation morph into hopelessness.

David encourages us. He thanks God for restoring him from more than one bout of hopelessness. By reading Psalm 23 slowly and savoring all it means, we soon anticipate our hopelessness being restored by God. Our praise of God returns as well.

The intent of this chapter is not to swallow our taste of hope too fast. Soul restoration begins by first dealing with the bitter taste of hopelessness and looking at from what God restores us.

DESCRIBING HOPELESSNESS

Describing hopelessness is harder than we think. I like Dr. Jerome Groopman's effort. He's a lead professor at Harvard Medical School and chief of experimental medicine at Boston's Beth Israel Deaconess Medical Center. He crafted his definition of hope from years of observing his patients.

> Although there is no uniform definition of hope, I found one that seemed to capture what my patients had taught me. Hope is the elevating feeling we experience when we see—in the mind's eye—a path to a better future. Hope acknowledges the significant obstacles and deep pitfalls along that path. True hope has no room for delusion.[1]

Using Groopman's method of observing others' experiences, I offer another definition of hopelessness that comes from observing David's life and reading his prayers. There are no delusions in them.

David's prayers are brutally honest. Four words in Psalm 23 summarize his experiences with hopelessness: "He restores my soul." Once we understand what David means by soul, we can grasp his experiences with hopelessness.

The Hebrew word for soul is *nephesh*, which means "life."[2] New Testament writers used Greek to segment life physically, emotionally, and spiritually. David reminds us they are intertwined.[3] Our physical or emotional drains can tax us spiritually, and our spiritual reservoirs can carry us through physical and emotional pain. All three influence our life.[4] When David says God restored his soul, he spoke of physical, emotional, and spiritual vitality.

David's use of *restore* doesn't refer to healing from physical pain or resolving everything stressing us. *Restore* means "to bring back."[5] We find it used in Old

---

1   Jerome Groopman, *The Anatomy of Hope: How People Prevail in the Face of Illness* (New York: Random House, 2004), xiv.

2   H. C. Leupold, *Exposition of the Psalms* (Columbus: The Wartburg Press, 1959), 211-212.

3   Albert Barnes, *Notes on the Old Testament: Psalms, Volume 1* (Grand Rapids: Baker Book House, 1870-72), 210-211.

4   Groopman, xvi.

5   John Phillips, *Exploring the Psalms: Psalms 1-88* (Neptune: Loizeaux Brothers, 1988), 176.

Testament law for making things right. If a cow was stolen or killed, the one responsible was to supply the owner with another cow (Leviticus 6:1-7).

David praises God for bringing his life back to its original condition with Him.[6] Many times, the circumstances around David didn't change, but the condition of his soul—his being—did. The word David uses elsewhere to describe his original state with God—and what he desperately wanted restored—is "joy."

David also used restore when Nathan the prophet confronted him about his marital affair with Bathsheba. David was immediately broken before God. Psalm 51 records his undiluted feelings and fears.[7] In one portion, David prays:

> *Create in me a clean heart, O God,*
> *And renew a steadfast spirit within me.*
> *Do not cast me away from Your presence,*
> *And do not take Your Holy Spirit from me.*

> *Restore to me the joy of Your salvation,*
> *And uphold me by Your generous Spirit.*
> *Then I will teach transgressors Your ways,*
> *And sinners shall be converted to You.*

—Psalm 51:10-13

Verse twelve unearths David's fear. The joy of his salvation had been robbed.[8] Verse eleven shows when David first experienced that joy—when Samuel anointed him as king and the Spirit of God came upon him (1 Samuel 16:13).

David's sin and circumstances had drained him of the joy of God's presence. That's what he wanted restored. That one aspect—the joy of God's presence—affected all areas of his life. If that was restored, then David's being, along with hope, would be restored.

---

6   Charles L. Allen, *God's Psychiatry* (New York: Jove/HBJ, 1978), 23.
7   Wiersbe, 191.
8   Ibid.

David's prayers in Psalms 23 and 51 are extremely descriptive. Observing them and David's life helps us describe hopelessness. Even as Jesus' followers, we experience traumatizing hopelessness like David's. At least now, using David's experience, we can describe it as mourning that our joy in Christ may never return.

Our joy in Christ influences all aspects of our lives. Joy is the word C. S. Lewis uses to describe his salvation and life in Christ. The former atheist writes, "Joy (in my sense) has indeed one characteristic, and one only, in common with them; the fact that anyone who has experienced it will want it again . . . I doubt whether anyone who has tasted it would ever, if both were in his power, exchange it for all the pleasures in the world. But then Joy is never in our power and Pleasure often is."[9]

Lewis is right. Joy is knowing God, through Jesus, has forgiven and adopted us. We are one with Him and He with us. Thus, Jesus says we experience complete joy through salvation (John 15:11). *Complete* means "joy-filled to the brim."[10] Nothing we can do will ever enable us to experience any greater joy than being in Christ.

Lewis is also right when he maintains that joy should consume every aspect of our lives. Once we have tasted it, we ache if we're not tasting it. If over time, we fear we'll never taste it again, our fear can turn into mourning. When we lose someone or something we dearly love, our emotions fluctuate between anger and sadness.

Finally, we have the full emotional description of hopelessness: mourning filled with grief and anger that our joy in Christ, which we experienced at salvation and that influenced all areas of our lives, may never return.

---

9   "Surprised by Joy Quotes," Goodreads.com, Accessed May 30, 2022, https://www.goodreads.com/work/quotes/877675-surprised-by-joy-the-shape-of-my-early-life.

10 The night before His crucifixion, Jesus taught His disciples, "I have spoken these things to you so that My joy may be in you and your joy may be complete" (John 15:11). The Greek word for "complete" is *pleroo* (play-ro'-o). Other synonyms for this word include "to cram," "to level up," and "to satisfy."

Although David has experienced hopelessness several times, God keeps restoring him. We can experience this, too, if we understand the causes of hopelessness.

CAUSES OF HOPELESSNESS

Hopelessness, like allergies, makes us miserable. I was tested for allergies twice as a child, once as a college student, and then once as an adult. As I grew, my allergies shifted. Growing up, I was more susceptible to dust and pollen. The last test revealed several food allergies and hurt worse—not by the way it was done but by what it revealed. I enjoy eating what it says I shouldn't.

Hopelessness has several causes. Like allergies, some may affect us at different times. Also like allergies, knowing what it does to us helps us take preventative steps. None of us likes the miserable feeling of hopelessness.

Ignorance contributes to hopelessness. When hopeless, we might think, "No one has ever experienced hopelessness as deeply as I do." As Christians, we can make it worse by thinking, "If I were a good Christian, I'd never feel hopeless. What's wrong with me?" Now their brownie of hopelessness has a guilt a la mode.

Feelings of hopelessness come with human nature, even for Jesus' followers. Moses, Elijah, and Jonah felt so hopeless that they asked God to kill them. David refers to multiple times of hopelessness in his life. Psalm 23 is filled with plurals. He pictures more than one green pasture and more than one place of still water God used to restore him.

Ignorance that hopelessness affects all of us can lead to deeper hopelessness. When feeling hopeless, we should see it as a season through which we all pass. And seasons are not permanent. They have a beginning and an end. Learning the other causes of hopelessness may help our season end quicker.

We often think sin alone leads to hopelessness. However, obedience can as well. Scottish-born theologian James Moffatt writes, "'He restoreth my soul' can have another meaning . . . 'He revives life in me.' Like a watch, the human spirit can just run down. We lose our drive and push. We become less willing to attempt the difficult."[11]

David prayed Psalm 142 at a low point in his life. Obedience landed him in the cave of Adullam. If we do what Jesus asks in our strength, we soon become the run-down watch. With nothing left, we complain to God and feel alone, abandoned, and hopeless.

Psalm 42:11 underscores how sin causes hopelessness as well. "Why are you cast down, O my soul? And why are you disquieted within me? Hope in God; For I shall yet praise Him, The help of my countenance and my God."

Noticing the influence of sin in this verse is difficult to see without help from Phillip Keller. According to Keller, "cast down" is a term shepherds use for sheep in a desperate state. If a sheep's wool becomes heavy or matted with mud or manure, the weight can topple it. Staying in that position for a long period can be fatal.[12] To protect them, the shepherd shears them. It's not a pleasant experience for either.

I watched my grandfather sheer sheep with his neighbor. Herding the sheep into the pen was difficult enough; but then they had to wrestle one away from the others, hold it down, and shear it. When finished, both my grandfather and the sheared sheep were happy the process was over.

Shearing is what David experienced in Psalm 51. God used the prophet Nathan to wrestle David away from his busy routine as king. When Nathan confronted him about his sin with Bathsheba, the shearing began.

David wept and confessed his sin to God. In time, David emerged from the shearing lighter and with renewed purpose. We hear it in verses Psalm 51:12-13. David tells God, "Restore to me the joy of Your salvation, And uphold me *by Your* generous Spirit. *Then* I will teach transgressors Your ways, And sinners shall be converted to You."

---

11   Allen, *God's Psychiatry*, 23.
12   Keller, 60-61.

Here, we see the various causes of hopelessness already mentioned. Un-shepherded activity causes hopelessness when we wander from God. Being an obedient sheep without being still with Jesus and drinking Him in leads to hopelessness. Being a disobedient, un-sheared sheep, whose life is matted by sin, leaves us feeling hopeless as well.

Sadly, we often stay that way because of another cause of hopelessness: misplaced trust. We keep looking for hope from sources that can never deliver it.

In 1999, Andrew Delbanco, professor of American Studies at Columbia University, wrote a short book entitled *The Real American Dream: A Meditation on Hope*. He identifies the collective hope of America in the eighteenth through the twentieth centuries. Delbanco defines the hope of a culture as what they collectively feel makes life meaningful. In the eighteenth century at the birth of our nation, God fulfilled this role. He was our collective Hope. By the nineteenth century, our hope in God had given way to hope in our nation. By the twentieth century, dissatisfied with both God and nation, America's collective hope became self. Our hope is in us.[13]

Two decades into the twenty-first century, many fear that individual hope will not produce shared hope. Some place their hope in the family, others in how much they can earn or acquire. Another group looks for hope in life experiences—where they go, what they do, or what they see. And some believe hope is discovered in philanthropy—giving ourselves away to help others.

We can also try to find hope by being accepted to a particular college, being cured of cancer, getting a job with good health benefits, having funds to pay the month's bills, or seeing our favorite team win a game.

The only hope with any lasting value was understood in the eighteenth century: God. David understood that if we are cast down, we need to put our

---

13   Timothy Keller, "Timothy Keller@HKU – Hope Beyond the Walls of the World," YouTube video, 1:21:15, https://www.youtube.com/watch?v=SD5LYJ3usoU.

hope in God. David's true hope was not found in defeating Goliath, escaping Saul, being crowned king, or overcoming the consequences of his sin. His hope—his joy—was never earned. Hope was given to him when Samuel anointed him as a ruddy shepherd-boy king. His joy was experiencing God's presence and doing His will.

When we place our hope in anything other than realizing God's presence and doing His will, we begin sliding into hopelessness. Other things may please for the moment, but they never secure continual joy.

Real hopelessness is not mourning that we'll not be healed, not get into our school of choice, not land our dream job, never see our children turn around, or never have our parents understand us. True hopelessness is mourning that our joy in Christ may never return.

THANK JESUS WHEN HOPELESS

My wife, Loree, was once bitten on her left index finger by a brown recluse spider. By the time we deduced the problem, the poison had entered the tendon sheath. Gangrene was spreading. It took four surgeries and over a year of physical therapy to recover her hand. During that time, she contracted chemical hepatitis and other unexpected complications.

I was a full-time pastor working on my Ph.D. Our boys were four and two. We were where God wanted us, doing what He asked. But the combination of so many taxing experiences left us depressed.

Then one day, Loree was listening to talk radio and heard a Christian counselor speak about David and the Psalms. He said the beauty of the Psalms is their honesty. They call a bad day "a bad day." They even describe why it's bad. Sometimes, the psalmist accepts responsibility for it; at other times, he blames others; and on occasion, he asks God, "Where are you?"

Then, the counselor added, "But regardless how bad the day or how hopeless the psalmist feels, you find him somewhere in the psalm praising God. It's remarkable how praising God leads you out of hopelessness."

Loree began practicing praise. Journaling her prayers, she found it difficult at first. Actually, she forced it. But over time, the praise became natural. After months, her praise was once again an overflow of her joy in Christ. Looking for ways and reasons to praise Jesus became her antibiotic—and mine—for hopelessness.

I wish I could say Loree and I have never experienced another hopeless day. But like David, we've learned those seasons can return, and we have gleaned lessons about the power of praise from those seasons.

First, thanking Jesus cuts away Satan's lies. In John 8:44, Jesus tells us Satan lies because that's his nature. Jesus calls him the "devil" in verse forty-four. It means "false accuser or slanderer." Even the label "Satan" means adversary. He's against anything God is for, especially believers following Jesus' lead in spreading the Gospel. Satan will lie to us about us, others, God, and circumstances. He does so to weaken us—to leave us feeling hopeless. And God purposes this so that we see the beautiful truths of God's presence, strength, and goodness as our Shepherd.

The best way to counter any lie is with the truth. Ephesians 6:17 describes truth as a weapon: the sword of the Spirit, which is God's Word. Other references to God's Word use the Greek word *logos*. Here, the Greek word *rhema* is used. It emphasizes the spoken word.

God knows our chief weapon against Satan's lies is to speak God's truth. What better way and time to do that than when we pray? We can speak the amazing truths about Jesus to Jesus.

- Jesus, thank You. I know I'm not the only one who has felt hopeless. You've restored others before. You've restored me before. You will restore me. Thank you (Psalm 23)!
- Jesus, You know all things. If this hopelessness is because of some sin in me, reveal it. Let me confess and repent of it. Thank You that I will experience renewed joy again (Psalm 51:10-13).

- Jesus, if this hopelessness is from the drain of following You in a hard season You purposed, thank You. You will give more to me today than I need to honor You with what You've purposed (2 Corinthians 9:8).
- Jesus, thank You that You are the true Source of my joy. Any other source is temporary and a lie. I trust You!

Second, thanking Jesus recalls God's nature. Thanking God when we become weak from following Jesus is proper. However, we can thank Jesus for even more.

Sometimes, our hopelessness stems from sin. We can thank Him for loving us enough to confront us over it. Hebrews 12:6 says God chastises those He loves. That's why He sent the prophet Nathan to confront David about his sin with Bathsheba. We'd rather avoid the pain when God convicts us of our sin. Instead, we need to thank Him for lovingly confronting us. Pain leads to restoration, and our restoration means fully and joyfully following Jesus again.

We can thank God for not giving up on us. David's joy of salvation came at Saul's expense. God removed His Spirit from King Saul and gave it to David. Because of Jesus' crucifixion, resurrection, and ascension, Jesus' Spirit fills us and never leaves us.

Part of our hopelessness comes from no longer feeling the joy of our salvation. Satan will tell us it's because Jesus has left us. But that's a lie. Our salvation is based on Jesus' grip on us, not our grip on Him. The grip is secure in His nature, not ours (John 10:25-30; Ephesians 1:13-14). Jesus' nature persists to glorify Himself to, in, and through us.

Third, thanking Jesus renews our hope. Department store entrepreneur J. C. Penney was once asked, "In one sentence, tell me the secret of your success in life." Penney quickly replied, "Here is the answer in four words: Adversity and Jesus Christ." Penney then explained that his father had been a poor preacher in the hills of Missouri. When he died, he left his children the following statement: "I bequeath you some honest debts, manly character, and faith in the Lord Jesus Christ."[14]

Penney's dad had left him an inheritance that carried him throughout life. Penney learned adversity is a part of life. Adversity can take away our money, our loved ones, and our health; but it can never take away our hope in Jesus.

Adversity is a constant in life. So is Jesus. When circumstances change, we can thank Jesus that He does not. He's not weaker or distracted. He's never broken a promise and is not about to start. His character "is the same yesterday, today, and forever" (Hebrews 13:8).

If I place my hope in circumstances, it will fluctuate from day to day. But when I place my hope in Jesus, regardless of what happens in life, my hope is secure.

14   Norman Vincent Peale, *The Rewards of Positive Living* (New York City: Open Road Media, 1981), 26-27.

CHAPTER SIX

LEAD ME IN RIGHT PATHS:
I NEED GUIDANCE!

He leads me in the paths of righteousness For His name's sake.

—Psalm 23:3b

THE LAST HALF OF VERSE three marks a shift in David's view of the Shepherd's care. In verse one, David praised God for meeting all his needs. In verse two through the first half of verse three, David boasted about the way God repeatedly revitalized him.

As Jesus' followers, we have reasons to boast as well. Today, God makes it possible for us to be still and drink in Jesus. And when we stubbornly press on, He makes us lie down, knowing we can't go on without being revived. He revives us, knowing we need it if we are to follow Him along the right paths.

I remember reading a *New York Times* article on "Decision Fatigue." It summarized the findings of a study that validated what we know to be true: making decisions is exhausting.

They ran a variety of tests to prove this. One took place at a mall. After learning about shoppers' experiences in the stores, the experimenters tested them with simple math problems. The participants could quit at any time. Researchers learned those who shopped more stopped sooner. Their conclusion: "When you shop till you drop, your willpower drops, too."[1] As the

---

1   John Tierney, "Do You Suffer from Decision Fatigue?" *The New York Times* online, August 17, 2011, http://www.nytimes.com/2011/08/21/magazine/do-you-suffer-from-decision-fatigue.html?mcubz=0.

number of decisions we make increases, our willingness and ability to make good decisions decreases.

Jesus, the Good Shepherd, knows we need to get still (lie down in green pastures) and drink Him in (He's our Still Waters), so He can revive us (restore our soul). We need that because each day forces us to make decisions. Not all are as weighty as others, but all take their toll. All affect our ability to discern, take, and stay on the paths of righteousness.

WHAT ARE PATHS OF RIGHTEOUSNESS?

Some paths are easier to take than others. It's easy to say yes to free airfare and reservations for a week at an all-inclusive resort. But we would likely think hard about giving up a week to sponsor thirty fifth graders on a mission trip in August to a hot, barren spot.

One of the more demanding decisions to make and keep is taking a righteous path. Such paths are normal to God, which makes them hard for us.

PATHS NORMAL TO GOD

The Hebrew word for "righteous," *tseh'-dek,* points to weights and measures.[2] It gives us the right value of a gold nugget or the right borders of an acre. Because these weights and measures are true for all, they are accepted as normal. The word is also used in Arabic to describe delicious dates. When looking at, touching, or eating a date, if nothing was wrong with it, they use this word to say, "Now, that's the way a date is supposed to be." It's normal. It's right.[3]

When David said God led him in paths of righteousness, he was talking about paths consistent with God's will and nature. They are the normal paths of God.[4] Though paths normal to God are amazing, they are difficult for us.

2 Francis Brown, S. R. Driver, and Charles A. Briggs, *The New Brown–Driver–Briggs–Gesenius Hebrew and English Lexicon, s.v.* "righteous" (Peabody: Hendrickson Publishers, 1979), 841.

3 Edmond Jacob, *Theology of the Old Testament,* trans. Arthur W. Heathcote and Philip J. Allcock (New York: Harper & Brothers Publishers, 1958), 94.

4 H. C. Leupold, *Exposition of the Psalms* (Columbus, Ohio: The Wartburg Press, 1959), 212.

God's righteous paths will be paths of justice. God will do what is right. He advocates for the helpless while holding the guilty accountable. Yet God's righteous paths will also be full of mercy. At times, He withholds what we deserve, even though we do nothing to deserve such kindness.

Although God's mercy and justice may seem random or inconsistent to us, they are normal to God and, in many ways, beautiful. Jesus displayed this while living on earth. Calling Jesus the "Word," John 1:14 asserts, "And the Word became flesh and dwelt among us, and we beheld His glory, the glory as of the only begotten of the Father, full of grace and truth." God's justice, mercy, and grace mix beautifully, naturally, and normally in Jesus.

Jesus never withheld grace to speak the truth. Ask the woman caught in adultery. After dispelling the crowd, Jesus told her what she had done was sinful and to stop. Also, ask the crowd surrounding her. While offering grace to her, Jesus confronted the self-righteous crowd about their sin (John 8:1-11).

I was once convicted to lead my church to live like Jesus: full of grace and truth. Before presenting this matter to the church, I shared it with Loree. She wisely said, "I know it is right, but doing so like Jesus will be difficult." As usual, she was right. What's normal for Jesus is hard for us. We don't naturally take the paths Jesus takes. That's why we must pray for His leading. But first, we need to acknowledge another reason why God's normal paths are hard for us.

PATHS THAT HONOR GOD'S NAME

David praises God for leading him "in paths of righteousness for His name's sake." Jews knew what this meant. A person's name then, like today, conveyed their character and reputation.[5] We see this when prospective parents pick a name for their newborn. Dad likes "Billy." But Mom rejects it: "I knew a Billy. He was horrible." When Mom suggests "Jack," Dad frowns. "No way. I grew up with a Jack who cheated at everything."

---

5   Ibid, 212.

Whether we accept it or not, our name becomes our brand and conveys who we are. We naturally long for paths consistent with our wants and nature. If the toll of a path requires any pain or strain, we'll pay it—as long as it helps our brand. We'll endure personal sacrifices and attacks if, in the end, it adds value to our reputation. We want people to say, "She gets things done," or "He's so humble and selfless."

David praised God for leading him down paths that were normal for God but not him. David thanked God for allowing him to promote God's reputation instead of his own.[6] It allowed him to have experiences he would have normally avoided. Praise also enabled David to see God's justice, mercy, strength, and goodness up close. A good example of this is David's bout with Goliath.

King Saul was head and shoulders taller than most men in Israel. Yet he refused to face Goliath. David, a fuzzy-faced freshman, confronted the nine-foot armored warrior. After Goliath growled about what he would do to David, David boldly replied:

> Then David said to the Philistine, 'You come to me with a sword, with a spear, and with a javelin. But I come to you in the name of the Lord of hosts, the God of the armies of Israel, whom you have defied. This day the Lord will deliver you into my hand, and I will strike you and take your head from you. And this day I will give the carcasses of the camp of the Philistines to the birds of the air and the wild beasts of the earth, that all the earth may know that there is a God in Israel. Then all this assembly shall know that the Lord does not save with sword and spear; for the battle *is* the Lord's, and He will give you into our hands'" (1 Samuel 17:45-47).

Although David walked from the battle with a giant's head in his hand and women singing songs about him, that was never his motivation. His

---

6   Robert T. Daniel, *How to Study the Psalms* (Westwood: Fleming H. Revell Company, 1953), 88-89.

confidence was in the name of the Lord of hosts.[7] David stood before the intimidating figure with impossible odds, not for his legacy but to honor the name of the Lord.

David experienced something others missed. David saw God at work in and through his life in ways others avoided—and all because he followed God's lead. Yet, the experience was so great that David thanked God for it and others like it, which he experienced later.

Another reason God's righteous paths are difficult is that they force us out of our familiar and comfortable ruts. According to Philip Keller, sheep are that way. He says, "Sheep are notorious creatures of habit. If left to themselves, they will follow the same trails until they become ruts; graze the same hills until they turn to desert wastes."[8]

Like sheep, we want our familiar, comfortable ruts. We want life predictable and manageable—even when our ruts are detrimental and don't feed us well. We get so much more from God and about God on His path. That's why David wrote more psalms than any others. He learned more about God on God's paths than in his ruts.

God's paths of righteousness are also taxing because He's the only One Who sees where they lead. I didn't know until researching that sheep have vision issues. They have great peripheral vision and can see what's beside and behind them. But they can only see ten to fifteen yards ahead.[9]

Most of us have vision issues, too. We remember experiences with God ten to twenty years ago, and we can describe what's happening in the world now. But none of us can say with confidence what the future holds. Only Jesus knows, which is why we must follow Him.

I only had three or four conversations with T. B. Maston, but I am amazed at how often I quote this revered professor of Christian ethics. He once told me God doesn't show us His detailed plan for our lives. He reveals it to us

7   F. B. Meyer, *Great Men of the Bible, Vol. 2* (Grand Rapids: Zondervan, 1982), 19-20.
8   Keller, 70-71.
9   Allen, 24.

76 PRAYING WITH DAVID

one path at a time. Only by obediently following Jesus on one path does God reveal the next path to take.

Most of us want all the details in advance. Where will I attend college? What will I do for a living? Will I marry? If so, who and when? Will I have enough saved to retire? These are common questions for blind, frightened sheep wanting life to be manageable. But righteous paths are far from clear and manageable for us. They are only that way to Jesus our Good Shepherd, which is why we must follow His lead.

HOW DOES JESUS LEAD?

David said God led him in the paths of righteousness, but that was not the first time David had talked about God's leadership. In verse two, he said, "He leads me beside the still waters." The Hebrew word translated "leads" is slightly different than in verse three.[10]

In verse two, we're being led for our well-being. It shows the Shepherd's care. The Shepherd knows we need strength, so He's leading us to still waters . . . to Himself so we can be revived.

Verse three differs. It highlights the Shepherd's purpose. He leads us for His benefit. He's taking us on a path for His name's sake. How Jesus leads us on paths of righteousness is very intentional.

G. Campbell Morgan discovered a side-effect of Jesus' leadership. The Hebrew word translated "leads" became a word Hebrews used for "sighing."[11] This leading by the shepherd was hard on the sheep. Their path was unfamiliar. Only the shepherd could see ahead. It was uncomfortable. He forced them from their usual ruts. The reason for doing this was unknown to the sheep and stressful. And though I've never seen or heard it, I can picture sheep giving a frustrated sigh.

We can relate. Jesus sometimes leads us on unfamiliar and uncomfortable paths. We're a healthy thirty-year-old who has been diagnosed with

10   Brown, 623-624.
11   Morgan, 58.

non-Hodgkin's lymphoma. We're skilled in IT and have been at the same company for twenty years but suddenly find ourselves unemployed. Or we're a Christian who spiritually dots all our *i*'s and crosses all our *t*'s, yet our child wants nothing to do with Jesus. These are unwanted paths.

An all-knowing God knew this was coming before we did and could have prevented it but didn't. God puts us here intentionally. Why? Before we begin looking for sins—and our sins can land us down unwanted paths—we should consider God's desire for all life: to glorify Him. We are on the path for His name's sake.

Even Jesus found Himself on an unfamiliar, unwanted, and uncomfortable path—His crucifixion. God placed our sins on Him. He became sin to God and experienced God's wrath because of us (Romans 5:8-9; 2 Corinthians 5:21; Matthew 27:46). On the night before His crucifixion, Jesus asked God for another path, one that might accomplish the same end—our salvation (Luke 22:39-42). Knowing this was the best way to glorify His name, God said no to Jesus. He had to follow God's path.

Jesus prayed for Himself, His eleven disciples, and those who would eventually experience salvation. And although praying for a different way to get it done, Jesus' aim above all was to glorify God. He mentioned it eight times in His prayer (John 17).

Jesus, our Good Shepherd, displays His glory by leading us to or not leading us away from unwanted paths. Like sheep, I often sigh to God over how hard, stressful, or painful the paths are; but it helps to remember Jesus' example. I need to be as intentional about displaying God's glory on my paths as Jesus was in displaying God's glory on His.

Hebrews 2:18 says that because Jesus was tempted and tested as we are, He can help us. The thoughts, fears, frustrations, and insecurities we have on hard paths, He had, too. That's why it's good He leads us personally. We are not alone on the hard path that displays Jesus' righteousness.[12] Jesus

---

12   Allen, 25.

goes before us and beside us and even models how to follow God on a strenuous path.

Remembering that our Good Shepherd goes before us reassures us. We can't see where the paths lead. We don't know if our illness will end with healing or Heaven. We cannot see the ones watching us on the journey. Nor do we know the ones along our path to whom Jesus wants to reveal His righteousness.

In the next chapter, we'll talk about the comforting touch of our Shepherd's rod and staff. Touches are tangible assuring expressions of the Shepherd's presence. Jesus shows us how close He is on our challenging paths. Those touches keep us following Him as He displays His righteousness.

PRAYING FOR GUIDANCE

Following Jesus' lead on the right paths doesn't turn hard paths into righteous paths. They are paths of righteousness because they display Jesus' righteousness. God uses such paths to reveal His justice, mercy, and grace. Because our nature is to avoid taxing paths, especially paths that benefit God over us, we need prayer. The prayers below help us follow Jesus and display His greatness on difficult paths.

Although we can't see where our path leads, how long it will take, or how it's displaying God's righteousness, we can look at it differently by changing our motivation. That's why David emphasizes that we follow these paths for the sake of God's name. Our every response to Jesus' lead reflects on Him. The prophets Jeremiah and Ezekiel emphasized that our response to God's lead either honors or profanes His name.[13]

Pray the following prayer: "Jesus, help me see this hard path differently. Remind me that You have given me this path to display Your righteousness today. Give me strength to honor Your name in what I say and by how I carry any physical pain or worries over the unknowns. Amen."

---

13 Daniel, 88-89.

As shared earlier, sheep can only see ten to fifteen yards in front of them. We, like sheep, want to see everything in advance. We want God to give us the full plan and even show us what He's doing and why.

I remember a time when I was discouraged. The pain of following Jesus had taken a toll. I was putting a lot of effort in but seeing no fruit. Whining to God in prayer, I said, "God, please show me a little fruit." I prayed that on a Monday morning. By Wednesday, He had uncovered so much fruit that I asked forgiveness. I prayed, "Father, forgive me. As long as You see the fruit, that is enough."

But still, I know my nature—our nature. We want details from God in advance, but our eyes cannot see what Jesus sees. Thus, I pray, "Help me trust You today with what You see, even though I can't see it. Lord, help me make Your ruts mine. Amen."

Sheep are creatures of habit. They like the same path. Over time, the path becomes a rut. The Hebrew word for "paths" can also be translated as "trench."[14] God's paths of righteousness are also well-worn ruts. The only difference is they are made by Him frequently traveling them. Remember, they are normal to God.

Knowing this, pray the following: "God, help me make Your ruts mine. Each day, by nature, I want to fall back to what's familiar, comfortable, and manageable. It's my familiar rut. Yet if I stayed there, there'd be little of my life that displayed Your righteousness. Help me follow Your lead today, accepting the path familiar to You over the one comfortable to me. Amen."[15]

In verse four, David mentions the comfort of God's rod and staff. The rod is for protection from predators. The crooked staff assures the sheep that if it falls, the shepherd can lift it back up on the path.

I need periodic touches from Jesus when following Him on a difficult path. An unexpected encouragement comes from a friend. A simple prayer

---

14   James Strong, *New Exhaustive Strong's Numbers and Concordance with Expanded Greek-Hebrew Dictionary.* (Nashville, Tennessee; Thomas Nelson, 2003), np, Biblesoft PC Study Bible One Touch Professional Series.
15   Keller, 73.

offered that morning is answered that afternoon. A verse from Scripture speaks specifically to my need.

The frequent small touches from God, touches that show how close He is, keep us on the path with Him. Therefore, pray, "Father, help me see, savor, and thank You for Your touches today. Knowing You are with me encourages me to keep following You, especially when I don't understand where You are leading me or why. Amen."

Phillip Keller helps me with this last prayer. The experienced shepherd writes, "A point worthy of mention here is that whenever the shepherd opens a gate into a fresh pasture the sheep are filled with excitement. As they go through the gate even the staid old ewes will often kick up their heels and leap with delight at the prospect of finding fresh feed. How they enjoy being led onto new ground.[16]

Like sheep, we like our familiar ruts. Like sheep, we can't see as far as the Shepherd and get nervous not knowing where Jesus' path will lead, how long it will take, or how draining it will be. Yet it helps to remind ourselves of the benefits of following Jesus.

One benefit is that our following Him will display His righteousness. We get to see the greatness of God. Another benefit is we can feed on rich, new pastures. Without Jesus' paths of righteousness, we eat from the same field, rehearsing the same truths and prayers. What we taste now is richer. Finally, we walk the new field close to our Shepherd. There's something priceless about being close to Jesus while on an adventure with Him.

Pray the following: "Father, remind me of all I get to experience on this new path with You. Although it's uncomfortable, I'll eventually taste new food—rich, new truths about You and me. I delight in having You close to me on this adventure. Amen."

---

16   Ibid, 74.

CHAPTER SEVEN

WALK WITH ME: I NEED COMFORT!

Yea, though I walk through the valley of the shadow of death, I will fear no
evil; For You are with me; Your rod and Your staff, they comfort me.

—Psalm 23:4

BELIEVERS WHO LIVE IN THE West often say, "The safest place is in the will of God." Followers of Christ in the East who are driven from their homes or martyred in record numbers disagree. David disagrees, too.

In verse three, David says God "leads [him] in the paths of righteousness for His name's sake." We learned in the previous chapter that righteous paths are natural to God, but not to us. God leads us on them to display His greatness to us and others. Righteous paths are always in His will. Although they honor Him, they are not always safe or comfortable.[1] That does not mean we cannot pray for God's comfort. David did in verse four.

Verse four highlights an often-overlooked shift in pronouns. Until now, David has been talking about Who God is and what He does for him.[2] Abruptly, David changes and begins talking to God. David assures himself by telling God how His rod and staff comfort him. David's change in pronouns assures him of God's comfort. Why? Because he knows we are either entering, experiencing, or leaving a dark valley we'd rather avoid.

---

1   Morgan, 59.
2   Phillips, 177.

We do a disservice when we say it's safe to be in God's will. Jesus tells us to expect hard valleys when following Him (John 15:20; 16:33). But from David's experience, we see how we can exit those valleys in awe of God. Not immediately sometimes. In time, as God sheds more light on our experience, we wind up worshiping Him—like David.

SHEDDING LIGHT ON DARK VALLEYS

When David thinks of his experience—his valley—he describes it as "the valley of the shadow of death." H. C. Leupold translates it as the "valley of deepest darkness."[3] The description conveys the darkest, most bitter experiences in life.[4] Some of our valleys are life-threatening. Others are life-draining. Then, some we create by envisioning all the horrible "what ifs" that haven't happened.

The phrase "shadow of death" comes from a compound Hebrew word conveying the most intense fear . . . the fear of death.[5] But not just any death. An "evil" death. Yet, David says he will fear no evil. Evil in the Old Testament projects a violent act or end.[6] This is important to know when reading how the "shadow of death" is used elsewhere in the Old Testament.

The Hebrew word for the "shadow of death" also appears in Job 28:3, describing the darkness of a mineshaft, and in Jeremiah 2:6, depicting a wild, uninhabited desert. But consider this: a mineshaft alone doesn't guarantee a violent death, nor does a desert. But staring at them, our mind naturally goes there. Before stepping into either, we've already produced a graphic movie trailer of how we will die. If not us, we stress over it happening to someone we love.

When our boys were in elementary school, Loree and I had a conversation with an older pastor and his wife who had grown children. Watching our

---

3   Leupold, 212-213.
4   Barnes, 211.
5   Karl Friedrich Keil and Franz Delitzsch, *Keil and Delitzsch Commentary on the Old Testament: New Updated Edition*, (Peabody: Hendrickson Publishers, Inc., 1996), electronic database.
6   Daniel, 90.

boys play, the wife told Loree, "My greatest fear in life was that something tragic would happen to one of my children. I just knew it would crush me." She continued, "But on the night our son was hit by a car, I found myself in the hospital, strong. God was with me, and He gave me what was needed to get through my greatest fear. That's when I learned that God doesn't give grace for 'what ifs.' But He does give you more than you need to get you through what He wants or allows."

Sometimes, we create our "valleys of the shadow of death." We walk them in our minds, without taking a step. The experiences are unknown, but the shadows of what could be have us thinking the worst. But truly, the worst would be going through it alone without our Shepherd. We forget Jesus' promises that will never happen (Matthew 28:20).

While touring Israel, our guide pointed to the mouth of a distant valley opening toward the sea of Galilee. He said, "That is the Valley of the Doves. Jesus and others traveled it to Nazareth." He added, "Though we don't see it, the Valley of the Shadow of Death in Psalm 23 was a real valley, too." Others describe it as a narrow, dangerous pathway weaving through the mountain ranges from the Dead Sea to Jerusalem.[7]

Although we envision some valleys, others we must walk through. They are hard and real. We walk them when we are diagnosed with ALS, our spouse files for divorce, our child goes to prison for life, we file for bankruptcy, or we hold our spouse for two years as cancer consumes them.

Phillip Keller experienced the last one with his wife. Walking through the unwanted valley together, Keller writes, "For two years we had walked through the dark valley of death watching her beautiful body being destroyed by cancer. As death approached, I sat by her bed, her hand in mine. Gently we 'passed' through the valley of death. Both of us were quietly aware of Christ's presence. There was no fear—*just a going on to higher ground.*"[8]

---

7   Allen, 27.
8   Keller, 84-85.

Whether we envision our valley or walk through it as Keller and his wife did, the effect is the same. It wears us down. Fear does that.

David mentions that while in his valley, he feared no evil. Keller said it, too. But why? Keller admits he and his wife "were quietly aware of Christ's presence." David says it as well in verse four. Jesus' presence makes all the difference.

THE POWER OF JESUS' PRESENCE

As explained earlier, David's pronouns change in verse four. He moves from talking *about* God to talking *to* God. And the "You" pronoun says a lot about God.

David opens his prayer with "the Lord is my Shepherd." "Lord" is the Hebrew *Yahweh*, meaning "the Great I AM." Other names for God in the Old Testament describe what God does: Healer, Provider, and Protector. Yahweh, however, focuses on Who God is and that He's relational.[9]

Why bring this up again? When we envision a foreboding valley before us or are overwhelmed by a real valley we are in, we often feel desperately alone. That's not true. Our greatest comfort is knowing Jesus, the Great I AM, is with us. As our Shepherd, He's equipped with His rod and staff. That was a comforting thought to David since he knew what that meant.

The shepherd's rod was intimidating. More like a club, they were about thirty inches long with nails around the head.[10] Remember, David told King Saul he had struck and killed both a lion and a bear (1 Samuel 17:34–35). Having a club helped. Now, David pictures God as His Shepherd beside him, ready to wield such a weapon.

I occasionally mention Jesus' rod and staff at a graveside. Because I have sat where they sit, we talk about the path they are on and the way Jesus uses His rod and staff. I tell them grief, like a lion, pounces without warning. It's hidden in a dresser drawer when we see a trinket of the one we love. It's waiting in the kitchen with the familiar smell of their favorite dish. Then like a bear, grief

---

9   Tony Evans, 44-45.
10   Herbert Lockyer, *All the Trades and Occupations of the Bible* (Grand Rapids: Zondervan, 1969), 201.

relentlessly mauls us. The ache lasts longer than we want. Thankfully, Jesus, the Good Shepherd, knows when grief is about to pounce and maul us. Like David, Jesus snatches us from the mouth of grief, not allowing it to consume us.

I experienced this our first Christmas without Dad, who always made us laugh. Although it had been seven months since his passing, it was our first Christmas without him. I envisioned it being quiet and lifeless. But as my brother and I placed the wrappings from ravaged gifts in the trash, it hit me. We laughed all night. The Shepherd had been with us.

Another tool in the shepherd's hand was his staff. More than a walking stick, the shepherd often needed the staff's crooked end. As Isaiah states, sheep tend to wander (Isaiah 53:6). The crook was used to pull them back to the shepherd.[11] Sheep also fell into ravines. When this happened, the shepherd hooked the flank of the sheep with the crook of the staff and lifted it back on the path.

When I read David's psalms, some record him wandering off and God pulling him back (Psalm 51). Others reveal his panicked bleating in a low place because of obedience (Psalm 142). All his psalms together show life as a mix of pain and praise of lows and lifts.

The safest place is not always in God's will. Following Jesus can lead to some low places. God leads us on righteous paths, not easy ones, and He does so for His name's sake.

Our assurance is knowing the Shepherd is beside us with staff in hand.[12] That was David's comfort. Not only does God want us to pray for comfort, but He also expects it.

PRAYING FOR COMFORT

David uses a Hebrew word for "comfort" that means to sigh or breathe.[13] Regardless of the depth of our low, knowing Jesus is our Shepherd

---

11 Barnes, 212.
12 Daniel, 90-91.
13 James Strong, *New Exhaustive Strong's Numbers and Concordance with Expanded Greek-Hebrew Dictionary*, s.v. "comfort" (Nashville, Tennessee; Thomas Nelson, 2003), np, Biblesoft PC Study Bible One Touch Professional Series.

comforts us. We breathe, knowing He's always with us with His rod and staff in hand. We experience that comforting breath each time we pray, asking Him to use them.

From what I have gleaned from verse four and personal experience, I want to prime your prayers for comfort with five of my own. Hopefully, they will encourage you when you find yourself in a low place.

THANK YOU, FATHER, THAT IT WILL NOT ALWAYS BE THIS WAY.

David passes through the valley. He doesn't stop or live in the valley. Even when Keller's wife endured terminal cancer for two years, they both knew it was a temporary valley. In time, she would pass through, as Keller says, "to higher ground."[14]

When Loree and I battled depression early in ministry, despair suffocated us. Family and friends loved us and prayed for us. Not until we met with a counselor who specialized in pastors experiencing depression did we finally breathe. He told us, "It won't always be like this." That short statement acted as Jesus' rod. It beat away our mauling despair. We were not whole yet, but we had been rescued from the bear's mouth. We breathed again.

Since then, we have shared those same words with others and watched them breathe. We should thank the Father that our valleys have an end date. Only God knows when it will be, but we know it will happen. Prayer helps us release what we know to be true.

FATHER, FIX WHAT I CAN'T.

David didn't pray this exact prayer, but he likely prayed something similar. Following David's biography in 1 Samuel, we find him in numerous inescapable positions. He was in a cave with Saul's army surrounding

---

14 Keller, 84-85.

WALK WITH ME: I NEED COMFORT!   87

him (1 Samuel 22:1-2). He was in enemy territory when his family and the families of all following him were abducted. The men closest to him considered killing him (1 Samuel 30:1-6). These small samples show David in valleys too deep and confusing for him to figure his way out. God had to fix his dilemma.

I have prayed that prayer when I was in what felt like a perfect storm. We've all had them—storms in our relationships, finances, or plans. Perhaps a combination of all three. I have looked at such times from every angle and tried different solutions, but the storm continued. Exhausted, I prayed, "Father, fix what I can't." Taking my hands off it, I saw the Father use His rod and staff. He comforted me while He fixed it.

Seeing God fix so many things I couldn't, I've learned to pray this prayer sooner rather than later. This also means my easy breathing comes sooner, too, and I experience His comfort.

JESUS, CALL ME BACK WHEN I WANDER OFF ON "WHAT IFS."

We make some of our valleys worse than they are by envisioning "what ifs." "What ifs" cast intimidating shadows, which make objects larger and more imposing than they are—just as "what ifs" do.

In the nineteenth century, Charles Haddon Spurgeon found a way to shed light on our shadows—our "what ifs." He wrote, "Nobody is afraid of a shadow, for a shadow cannot stop a man's pathway even for a moment. The shadow of a dog cannot bite; the shadow of a sword cannot kill; the shadow of death cannot destroy us. Let us not, therefore, be afraid."[15]

Asking Jesus to hook us with His staff when we wander or focus on the "what ifs" is important. We need Him to draw us close. From His side, we see everything from His perspective. Now comforted, we breathe easier.

---

15   Spurgeon, 110.

*JESUS, LIFT ME FROM MY EMOTIONAL
PIT AND CARRY ME A WHILE.*

This prayer comes from the image Jesus gives in Luke 15:3-7. Telling the parable of a lost sheep, Jesus says once the shepherd finds it, he puts it on His shoulders and carries it home.

Jesus' story describes what happens when one repents, but I need that same feeling at times as a stressed sheep. Walking through a hard valley, I'd like to sense Jesus picking me up and carrying me on His shoulders for a while.

Loree and I experienced this early in our ministry. We had served a challenging church during a demanding season. That's when the depression I mentioned earlier surfaced. I was thirty-two and wanted to leave the ministry. But God made some changes in our lives, and for the next year, Jesus carried us. Not only was I restored that year, but I was also recharged and eager to continue following Jesus in ministry.

But I offer one caution. When asking Jesus to carry us a while, we shouldn't assume He will carry us our entire life. We are not entitled to a comfortable ride. Our role as His sheep is to follow Him—even in deep, exhausting valleys—which is where we see His greatness the most and where He displays it to others through our circumstances.

*FORGIVE ME FOR FORGETTING
THE GREAT I AM IS WITH ME.*

We can pray any number of prayers when we need comfort, but in all of them, we need to remember who's walking with us. Yahweh, the Great I AM, is our Shepherd. Regardless of how weary we feel in following Him, we're not carrying as much of the load as He is.

My dad once gave me this picture through a story. When he was a boy, his stepdad asked him to help carry a log across a field. At only ten years old, Dad picked up the end of the log. Halfway across the field, Dad's young legs quivered beneath the weight. Seeing this, his stepdad said, "Charles, let's stop and take a break." Glad to drop his end of the log, Dad looked back and was surprised. His stepdad wasn't at the other end. He was in the middle carrying most of the weight.

When I feel the weight of my valley is too much, when I want to stop and drop my end, I remember Dad's tale. Regardless of how drained, discouraged, or hopeless I feel, Jesus still carries the heaviest end of the load. I have the Great I AM with me. With Him, I have more than I need to get through the valley.

Being in God's will is *not* the safest place. Jesus will lead us into valleys where only He knows the way through and how long it will take. The reason we are there has nothing to do with us but everything to do with God displaying His greatness to us and others.

Yet being in God's will is the *best* place to be. There, we experience an amazing journey with our Good Shepherd. We see Him use His rod and staff to comfort us or, if needed, to place us on His shoulders for a while. Only then do we observe firsthand how great He is because of how much we depend on Him. In the valleys, we grow closer to the One leading us through the valleys and comforting us in them.

CHAPTER EIGHT

GO BEFORE ME: I NEED PEACE!

You prepare a table before me in the presence of my enemies.

—Psalm 23:5a

DEEP TRUTHS COME FROM DEEP places. We simply don't want to be in a deep place—a hard, confusing, hopeless, frustrating place—to learn them. David does that for us. From David's deep places in life, we learn the following:

- **The source of anger is fear.** Fear is the chief reason we get angry at God, ourselves, or others. Specifically, it's the fear of pain or disappointment.

- **The counter to fear is trust.** Trusting Jesus, even with a painful unknown, dramatically calms our fears.

- **The prompter of trust is prayer.** Prayer is a proven vehicle, enabling our trust in God to calm our fears.

- **The result of prayer is peace**. Confronting our fears in prayer strengthens our trust in God. As in any relationship, trust requires constant communication, and trust is synonymous with peace.

- **The effect of peace is faithfully following Jesus, even in a hard valley.** This is why Jesus, our Good Shepherd, prepares tables for us amid our greatest fears. He wants us to follow Him. Only then do we and others see His glory.

Fortunately, I married a reader. She once read that the underlying source of anger is either pain or fear. If it's true, a lot of pain and fear reside beneath what seems to be a sweeping epidemic of anger. We see the epidemic growing in the escalating cases of domestic violence, child abuse, road rage, and riots. These show when anger erupts. Yet when listening to mainstream media or reading social media, we sense the lava of anger smoldering beneath the surface.

If what Loree read is correct, a lot of pain or fear simmers in most of us. Thus, we need to talk more about managing our fears than our anger. Addressing our fears cools the anger within. David does this. Although this doesn't sound like an effective fear-managing tool, it is.

As an experienced shepherd, David knows the power of his metaphor. He thanked God for providing a table—a place of rest and peace on a fearful path. Understanding the metaphor as David intended helps us greatly because it surfaces our constant need for a table. We frequently need peace because we're often scared. The peace comes easier when we realize Jesus, our Shepherd, prepares our tables in advance.

But how does knowing this address our fears? Psalm 56 tells us. David had been captured by his enemies, the Philistines. The psalm records his prayer for peace when he was consumed with fear. Though Psalm 23 describes the peace Jesus provides, Psalm 56 shows how to pray to experience it.

NEEDING A TABLE

I chuckled reading Chuck Swindoll's chapter on anger in *Three Steps Forward Two Steps Back*. He quotes Thomas Jefferson who said, "When angry, count to ten before you speak; if very angry, a hundred." Seventy-five years later, Mark Twain revised Jefferson's words: "When angry count four. When very angry, swear."[1]

Some are so angry today, they don't even count one before cursing. But again, it's not an anger issue. Anger is the symptom. The source is fear. When

---

1   Charles R. Swindoll, *Three Steps Forward Two Steps Back: Persevering through Pressure* (Nashville: Thomas Nelson Publishers, 1980), 149.

consumed with fear, David prescribed our need for a table—not a dining or kitchen table, but the green pastures talked about in verse two of Psalm 23.

To better understand David's metaphor, we must tie verses four and five to verse two. Verse four references walking "through the valley of the shadow of death." This was a real valley, extending from the Dead Sea to Jerusalem. Scholar F. B. Meyer implies it could have passed through Bethlehem where David tended sheep, making David familiar with it.[2]

From the Dead Sea to Jerusalem, the dangerous valley ascends three thousand feet. Those who have visited Israel may have seen the deeply cut mountains leading to Jerusalem. That means shepherds like David knew of various tables along the way. "Tables" was a shepherd's term for plateaus or mesas pressed in a mountain range.[3] They were a perfect place for sheep to rest, especially when migrating through a dangerous valley.

When we add verse two, we get a powerful picture. The Good Shepherd makes us lie down in green pastures. Sheep need rest to digest what they've already eaten. Even when in a hard and frightening valley, Jesus knows we need to stop and digest important truths. We need to remember we are not alone. The Great I AM is with us. Our Good Shepherd is not weak or suddenly distracted. His character has not changed, and He's equipped with His protective rod and assuring staff. If we fall, He will lift us.

When in a difficult valley, all we see are the real or imagined dangers. We need to stop and digest what's true so we can replace our fears with peace.

Some valleys are more fearful than others because we've traveled them before. The doctor tells us our cancer has returned. We learn our company is going through another re-organization. We see signs our loved one is addicted again. Any valley we've passed through before increases our fear of traveling it again.

---

2   Meyer, 12.
3   Keller, 104-105.

Some time ago, our niece, her husband, and their two preschool-age boys were in an automobile accident. An eighteen-wheeler didn't see them in the lane to his left. Changing lanes, the truck forced Jake into the grassy median. Their car rolled several times before stopping in the lane of oncoming cars. Gratefully, they were not hit by other cars. Although Jake required staples to the back of his head and April needed stitches on her leg and foot, the two boys emerged with only scrapes and bruises.

Accidents like this cause more than physical wounds. One of the boys relived the experience. Each time he described it, he said, "I saw the grass, then the sky. I saw the grass, then the sky. Then, we crashed." Later when his dad and mom were ready to head home again, he wasn't. His greatest fear was getting into the car and traveling the same road on which they had crashed.

Often, our past experiences create future fears. We don't want to go down that road again. But David reminds us that his Shepherd prepared a table in the presence of his enemies. When surrounded by our greatest fear or when reliving a painfully familiar road, our Shepherd can cause us to rest. Jesus gives peace amid our greatest fears because He knows where the tables are. In fact, He prepares them.

THE SHEPHERD'S PREPARATION

In our marriage, Loree is the gifted host, and I'm her un-hired hand. Because of her, I know about the advance prep-work involved in preparing for family or friends who eat or stay with us.

The same is true of Jesus. Our all-knowing Good Shepherd knows when He'll lead us through a hard valley. He also knows how long it will take and when we need to stop to regain strength from Him.

During a visit to Israel, I rode from the Dead Sea to Jerusalem, which took around two hours. Our airconditioned tour bus made it enjoyable. For shepherds like David, however, the trip was longer and more difficult. They led their herds for miles through a slithering valley that ascended three thousand feet and was filled with predators and ravines. Thus, they needed to prepare a lot of tables. Jesus does the same for us.

Experienced in leading sheep, Philip Keller describes how he prepared for leading them on a long journey. He first took the trip himself, reviewing where the tables (plateaus) were and what needed to be done.

Then, just before they started the journey, he returned to the tables to prepare them. Some had watering holes. He cleaned them of fallen debris and removed any poisonous plants. Sheep can be indiscriminate eaters. Finally, Keller surveyed the mesa, looking for signs of predators—specifically, lions.[4]

We can translate this into what Jesus does for us. He knows our valleys in advance and when and where we will need rest. Sometimes, our tables are "getaways." Like the shepherd who removes poisonous plants from the sheep's grazing areas, Jesus leads us to a place of fewer temptations, distractions, burdens, and fears. Then, we can lie down beside the still waters. When we are still, we can see, hear, rest, and find strength in Jesus alone.

These table places also give us a respite from Satan's attacks. Peter describes Satan as a prowling and roaring lion who looks for anyone he can devour (1 Peter 5:8). I've experienced tables with Jesus where He dispelled the lies Satan told me. Lies about me, others, my valley, and my life with Jesus.

But I also know my nature and human nature. Panicked over our valley and looking for a way out, we often ignore the tables Jesus prepares. We don't want to stop and rest in Him. We just want out of the valley. We forget God puts us in the valley to honor Him and display the beauty of who He is to us and an observing world. Jesus, the Good Shepherd, helps us do that by providing tables along the way. They restore us so we can continue honoring Him as we follow Him through the valley.

Sometimes, we might wonder if Jesus understands how stressful our valleys are. He does. He had to travel them in advance to make the tables possible. His preparation of our tables came at a cost.

4   Keller, 105.

If Keller saw lion tracks, he was prepared to face the lion on behalf of the sheep. Jesus went through all He faced to walk with us through our valleys. Psalm 22 fittingly precedes Psalm 23. Before David talked about the Good Shepherd in Psalm 23, he prophetically depicted Jesus' sacrifice in Psalm 22. A thousand years before Jesus' crucifixion, David wrote in Psalm 22:12–18:

> *Many bulls have surrounded Me;*
> *Strong bulls of Bashan have encircled Me.*
> *They gape at Me with their mouths,*
> *Like a raging and roaring lion.*
>
> *I am poured out like water,*
> *And all My bones are out of joint;*
> *My heart is like wax;*
> *It has melted within Me.*
> *My strength is dried up like a potsherd,*
> *And My tongue clings to My jaws;*
> *You have brought Me to the dust of death.*
>
> *For dogs have surrounded Me;*
> *The congregation of the wicked has enclosed Me.*
> *They pierced My hands and My feet;*
> *I can count all My bones.*
> *They look and stare at Me.*
> *They divide My garments among them,*
> *And for My clothing they cast lots.*

Walking our valley consumed with fear, we wonder if Jesus understands and cares about what we're going through. We forget what He went through to face the lion head-on. He defeated Satan and also satisfied God's wrath against our sin.

That's why I believe Jesus commands His sheep to regularly observe the Lord's Supper. At this table, we remember all He did to prepare our spiritual rest in Him. This solemn memory inspires us to honor and trust Him in the valleys.

PRAYING FOR PEACE

Fear also tempts us to run past the tables Jesus prepares. How do we resist doing so? What does it take for us to stop and rest in Jesus, especially when surrounded by our fears? I learned when I was five that it takes trust and prayer.

On a night when lightning and thunder competed for attention, the local weatherman announced we were under a tornado watch. Jumping from my bed, I ran to Dad and said, "Daddy, I'm scared."

He drew me close in a comforting squeeze. With a calm voice, he said, "Mark, repeat after me, 'What time I am afraid, I will trust in thee.'" I repeated it two or three times, and Dad said, "Son, trust God. He'll take care of you."

I went back to bed quoting Psalm 56:3 until I fell asleep. Decades later, this verse still comes to mind many times, and I quote it, remembering the greatest counter to my fears is trusting Jesus.

I now know more of the story behind David's prayer in Psalm 56. It comes from his experience in 1 Samuel 21 where he acts insane outside the gates of Gath to escape capture and death. In Psalm 56:1-4, David confesses His extreme fear but trust in God. The remainder of the psalm models how prayer moves us from fear to trust and from trust to peace when walking through a valley.

Some of the more frightening aspects of our valleys are the looming thoughts, words, and actions of others. David prays in verses five through seven:

All day they twist my words;
All their thoughts are against me for evil.
They gather together,
They hide, they mark my steps,
When they lie in wait for my life.

Shall they escape by iniquity?
In anger cast down the peoples, O God!

I remember the "holler" behind my grandparents' back gate. Holler is Texas-speak for a small, wooded valley. I dreamed of exploring it during the day but never at night. Picture two adjacent hills competing for space. The winding, ribbon-like path between them acted as a referee. Green underbrush and fallen rock crowded the path like taunting stones tossed by each hill. That's why I never ventured up the holler at night. Too many threatening unknowns.

Our valleys intimidate us the same way. We feel them in the threatening subtleties or the bullying opinions and actions of others. Whether during the day or at night, our valley immobilizes us with fear. All we want to do is stand and scream, which isn't a bad idea. David does that in verses five through seven. Only he is screaming to God.

David lets his fears breathe by identifying them. He tells God he's tired of others' misconceptions about him. He's fed up with how people twist his words and plot his demise. David releases all that he's feeling and says, "You take care of them."

We sometimes must walk the dark "hollers" created by those who don't fear God. Although we don't like their actions, we should expect them. They're acting the way people without a relationship with Jesus act. But what if God's people are the cause of our dark holler? What if their disobedience to God has made our valley more difficult?

Macel Falwell's biography of her husband, Jerry Falwell, talks about this. She said Jerry was not hurt by the attacks from non-Christians. The wounds were deeper and the weight heavier when the attacks and criticism came from fellow Christians.[5]

We should do the same when attacked or wounded by fellow believers as we do with nonbelievers—speak the truth. But when it's a group, church, or denomination, we can give them to God and ask Him to address them.

---

5   Macel Falwell, *Jerry Falwell: His Life and Legacy* (New York: Howard Books, 2008), 40.

David's second prayer helps him rest because he acknowledges God's sovereignty (vs. 8–9).

> *You number my wanderings;*
> *Put my tears into Your bottle;*
> Are they *not in Your book?*
> *When I cry out to You,*
> *Then my enemies will turn back;*
> *This I know, because God* is *for me.*

When reeling from the fatiguing aches and fears of our valley, we should pray: "God, I trust you. You not only have a record of my valley, but also of my tears. You know what I'm walking through because You are with me, and Your rod and staff comfort me (Psalm 23:4). Because Your Spirit is within me, You know what I'm thinking and feeling (John 14:15–17; 2 Corinthians 2). I trust you. You've purposed this valley to display Your glory to me and others. You've provided tables to assure me of Your presence and care and to restore my soul (Psalm 23:3). Although I don't like this valley—and though I want out of this valley—I trust You. You know what You are doing. I will keep following You."

Instead of playing insane, David could have compromised God's calling by saying, "God told me I was to be king. I've been faithful to King Saul for years. Yet, he is still king, and I'm a fugitive. I quit. I'd rather live as I want than struggle obeying what God wants."

David could have done what many of us are tempted to do in a valley—compromise God's Word. David chooses the opposite in verses ten and eleven:

> *In God (I will praise His word),*
> *In the* Lord *(I will praise His word),*
> *In God I have put my trust;*
> *I will not be afraid.*
> *What can man do to me?*

David has a greater fear of disobeying God's Word than of disappointing others. He had a greater fear of walking out of the valley and doing what he wanted than he did of staying with God in the valley and following His Word and leading.

The pain of hard valleys tempts every believer to compromise God's Word. A new job with higher pay and better benefits tempts us to lie on our resume and application. Growing debt from acquiring things beyond our means tempts us to restrict what we give to God. Fear of being rejected tempts us to lower biblical values to keep relationships.

But to endure the valley, to come through it fulfilled by the journey and with a deeper appreciation of Who God is and what He does, we must trust in God's Word. That means knowing and doing nothing more and nothing less than what He says.

One benefit of stopping at a table with Jesus is that it reminds us of past valleys and tables with Him. In verses twelve and thirteen, David praises God. His prayer became an encouraging reminder to him and us of God's faithfulness in our valleys.

Vows made to You are binding upon me, O God;
I will render praises to You,
For You have delivered my soul from death.
Have You not kept my feet from falling,
That I may walk before God
In the light of the living?

David was still a fugitive from Saul. He didn't know when he would be king. But fresh off an amazing experience with God, David praised Him. Praising God at the table, remembering what God has just done, David was restored to continue following Him in the valley.

Value resides in reflecting on past valleys and tables and praising God. Remembering all He has done in our past gives us the trust and peace to continue with Him. Even if we don't know how long the valley will be or when the next table will come, we can trust God and keep following.

A REMINDER FROM PAUL

Following are the deep truths I hope we will take home from our time with Psalm 23:5:

- The source of anger is fear.
- The counter to fear is trust.
- The prompter of trust is prayer.
- The result of prayer is peace.
- The effect of peace is faithfully following Jesus, even in a hard valley.

Philippians 4:4–7, one of my favorite passages in Scripture, speaks to the above conclusions. Paul was in jail and writing to fellow followers in Philippi. The prisoner tries to calm and encourage those worried about him. Paul's tone reflects that he was writing like a sheep resting peacefully at a table prepared by his Shepherd, and he wants his friends to experience that same peace. He says, "Rejoice in the Lord always. Again I will say, rejoice! Let your gentleness be known to all men. The Lord *is* at hand. Be anxious for nothing, but in everything by prayer and supplication, with thanksgiving, let your requests be made known to God; and the peace of God, which surpasses all understanding, will guard your hearts and minds through Christ Jesus."

Paul experienced what David had. He encouraged the Philippians and us to do the same. Calm down. Stop and pray. Trust God. He's already ahead of us preparing the way. Thank Him. Rest in Him. Breathe. Experience and display His peace. Such peace when surrounded by our greatest fears is an act of worship. It also displays to others the difference God makes.

CHAPTER NINE

SHOW ME WHAT I HAVE: I NEED CONFIDENCE!

You anoint my head with oil; My cup runs over.

—Psalm 23:5

MY SON, JOHN MARK, ONCE asked me to run the Monument 10K (6.2 miles) with him. It's an annual event in Richmond, Virginia. He gave me advance notice, so we could train. But I wouldn't call running four times in two months "training," especially when it was a mix of running, walking, and talking. Still, we joined twenty-six thousand other runners and ran.

He and I finished the race together—but differently. He was all smiles. I looked for a chair. He stayed and enjoyed the exhibits surrounding the race. I went home, took two pain pills, put ice on my knees, and went to bed.

And one more difference. John Mark practically sprinted the last tenth of a mile. I struggled to resemble a runner. He could have easily gone farther. I thought, *There's no way I'd ever do a half-marathon—13.1 miles.*

Following Jesus puts us on righteous paths—paths that fit His nature, not ours. He even leads us through frightening valleys. Taxed from either an unnatural path or an unwanted valley, we lose all confidence to go farther. That's why we need the last half of verse five. David was a weary sheep; but his Shepherd "anoint[ed his] head with oil," and "[his] cup [ran] over."

As a shepherd, David knew what the oil and cup meant to sheep. The oil represented healing and the cup reviving. For us, it means more. Jesus' Spirit within us is our healing oil and reviving water. Knowing this, we regain the confidence not only to complete our current path or valley but also to sign up for the next valley, path, or race with Jesus.

HEALING OIL

I once thought David was recalling Samuel anointing him as king (1 Samuel 16:13), but that wasn't something so nostalgic or noble. As a young shepherd, David carried oil with him to heal the sheep from small threats and fresh wounds. Rather, David thanked God for healing him repeatedly from his threats and wounds. We, too, gain spiritual health when we stop and thank God—even for healing and protection from small threats.

Our friend Phillip Keller identifies summertime as "fly time." During the summer season, various flies attach sheep and other livestock.[1] The nose fly is among the worst. It deposits eggs in the sheep's nose. If untreated, larvae hatch in a few days and move up the nasal passage. Seeking relief, sheep rub their heads on the ground or beat them against trees and rocks. Advanced stages of infection cause blindness. Severely distraught, the sheep stop eating. Some die.[2]

To protect his sheep from such flies, Keller smeared a homemade remedy composed of linseed oil, sulfur, and tar on the sheep's head and in its nose.[3] We don't know what homemade remedy David used; but no doubt, oil was in it. On one of my trips to Israel, our Israeli guide pointed to shepherds tending sheep. He reported that, as David did long ago, they use oil to protect the eyes, ears, and nose of the sheep from flies.

David thanks God for protecting him from the small threats that in time could consume him. Although the list of such threats is long and can vary, I

---

1   Keller, 114.
2   Ibid, 115-116.
3   Ibid, 116.

identified seven in a series of lessons called, "Dangerous Molehills." This was my creative way of saying that if we don't address these when small, they can become mountain-size problems. They include the unbridled tongue, unchecked pride, unprotected eye, unrenewed mind, unappreciated gift, unreconciled hurt, and undisciplined life.

God addresses each of these and more in His Word. As vulnerable sheep, we need to approach our Good Shepherd and be still with Him and His Word. He will apply the oil to protect us from small threats before they become large.

The shepherd's oil also protects the sheep from infection.[4] When migrating, sheep can be cut by sharp stones or pricked by briars. At the end of the day, the shepherd examines each sheep for open wounds. He applies oil to prevent infection.[5]

Many of us carry open life wounds that are sensitive to the touch. Like physical wounds, emotional and spiritual wounds occur for different reasons and have different depths and lengths. The only One Who sees them and can doctor them is Jesus, our Good Shepherd. Sadly, for various reasons, we will not let Him apply the oil. Simon Peter was like that.

Peter did what He never thought he would. He denied Jesus. Not once, but three times. During various appearances by Jesus after His resurrection, Peter didn't bring it up. Jesus finally confronted him with it in John 21. Jesus asked Peter three times, "Do you love me?" This touched Peter's wound because it was the same number of times he had denied Jesus. Reliving the moment, Peter wept in pain and said, "Lord, you know all things; You know that I love you" (John 21:17).

Like a shepherd with a wounded sheep, Jesus singled out Peter and brought him close so He could address and heal his wound. But why didn't Peter seek Jesus? Why didn't Peter seek healing? Maybe for the same reasons we don't. Following are three possibilities:

---

4   Allen, 32.
5   Leupold, 213-214.

- **Like Peter, we don't feel we deserve healing**. Our wound was our fault, and we must carry its pain as penance. The way Jesus confronts Peter to heal him shows how silly this attitude is. Jesus seeks to heal wounds. Doing so enables us to follow Him. As we follow Him, Jesus displays His glory to us and through us to others.

- **Like Peter, we fear the healing process will be too painful**. We don't want Jesus to confront us with it. We don't want to relive it or go through the "spiritual therapy" with Him for healing. With a physical wound, physical therapy is harder and longer than the surgery. Spiritually and emotionally, we'd rather carry our current pain than risk any deeper pain.

- **Like Peter, we know healing will remove our reason for not following Jesus more closely**. Each time Peter reaffirmed his love for Jesus, Jesus gave him a job. Amusingly, Jesus described each job in shepherd's terms. He tells Peter to feed His lambs (v. 15), to shepherd His sheep (v. 16), and to feed His sheep (v. 17). But after describing Peter's future painful death, Jesus told him to follow Him (v. 19).

These three possibilities give us compelling reasons to avoid healing, so why would we want Jesus to heal our wounds? The best reason is that Jesus does it. Why wouldn't we want His personal touch and mentoring? We'd learn so much more about Him and ourselves in the process. Why wouldn't we want to be healed so we could follow Him more and see and display more of His greatness? Whether through His healing or in our following, we get the benefit of drinking from His cup.

REVIVING CUP

Our Israeli guide also said some shepherds referred to their feeding or watering trough as "the cup." I like Charles Allen's description better: "The shepherd had a large earthen jug of water, the kind of a jar which kept the water refreshingly cool through evaporation. As the sheep came in, the shepherd would dip down into the water with his big cup and bring it up brimful. The tired sheep drank deeply."[6]

Drained from following the shepherd, the sheep saw the earthen jar. They knew from experience what was inside. Even if there had been no rain, they knew the shepherd always had it full. Whether the journey that day had been long or short, hard or easy, the sheep saw the jar and cup. They knew their shepherd always had more than they needed.

I was reminded of this in one of my favorite verses: "And God *is* able to make all grace abound toward you, that you, always having all sufficiency in all *things*, may have an abundance for every good work" (2 Corinthians 9:8).

This verse became a favorite after reading the autobiography of Bertha Smith. The single, twenty-eight-year-old arrived in China on September 4, 1917. The next youngest member of her team was over forty. Early on, she buried herself in learning the language and customs. Seeing the children there, she longed to be married and have children of her own. But God said no. Less than two years later, she received word her dad had died.

By the summer of 1920, Smith was a wounded, dehydrated sheep. That's when Dr. Charles G. Trumbull arrived.[7] He reminded Smith of her Shepherd's cup. Dr. Trumbull pointed Smith to passages describing the greatness of God. She spent two weeks drinking from one verse alone: 2 Corinthians 9:8. Swallowing the cool water of each word, Smith emerged refreshed and revived. Below is how each word tasted to her:

> *God*—The living, all-knowing, all-loving, ever-present One deserved my constant adoration and worship.

> *Is*—God here and now is all that he ever has been!

> *Able*—He is the all-powerful One who spoke the universe into existence. Certainly he is able to do for me all that I can ever need.

---

6   Allen, 32.
7   Bertha Smith, *Go Home and Tell* (Nashville, Tennessee: Broadman Press, 1965), 1-7.

To make—God, having created all from nothing, can make that which does not exist in order to supply my need. He "calleth those things which be not as though they were" (Romans 4:17). He will make all things work together for my good (Romans 8:28).

All grace—That which is the favor of God; I cannot by any effort merit it. It being God's free gift, I can only accept it. God gives not just enough grace for one specific need, but all grace, every kind of loving favor sufficient for every situation.

Abound—There would not be just enough strength, wisdom, and patience to get by, but abundance which could never give out.

Toward you—To whom? "God is able to make all grace abound toward you," which means me! Regardless of any lack I may have in natural ability and gifts, that grace abounds toward me. I can take it according to my need.

To every good work—Why is such abundant grace given to me? Is it that I sometimes may do a little service for him? It is that I may always serve him! How? Am I just to serve in my own human weakness? No! I, always having all sufficiency in all things, may abound to every good work.[8]

Dr. Trumbull gave Smith an exercise that helped her grasp the cup more quickly in the future. He taught her not to sing "I Need Thee Every Hour" but rather "I Have Thee Every Hour. Oh, I have Thee." She said it made all the difference.[9]

We have repeatedly said that Jesus is our Good Shepherd (John 10). In John 14:15–18, Jesus assures us that He is always with us: "If you love Me, keep My commandments. And I will pray the Father, and He will give you another Helper, that He may abide with you forever—the Spirit of truth, whom the

---

8   Ibid, 7-8.
9   Ibid, 8.

world cannot receive, because it neither sees Him nor knows Him; but you know Him, for He dwells with you and will be in you. I will not leave you orphans; I will come to you."

With Jesus' Spirit in us, we have all that He is and promises. That may be why David referred to the cup later in his reflective prayer rather than at the beginning.

David began by seeing the Great I Am as his Shepherd. Then, he reflected on having a Shepherd Who made him lie down for rest, strengthened him with cool water, restored him with hope, led him on the right paths, and comforted him when he was frightened. He even healed David's hurt. No wonder David said, "My cup runs over."

We have the Spirit of Jesus, our Good Shepherd, living within us every hour. We can pray to Jesus and sing about Him with the same awe and gratitude as David.

CONFIDENCE-BUILDING PRAYER

On some days, feeling that our cups run over seems more difficult. That's when prayer helps. To experience the benefit of Jesus' presence, His healing and reviving, we can tweak our payers. I offer three suggestions.

FATHER, REMIND ME THIS IS ONLY A SEASON.

The frustrating flies only last for a season. Keller's sheep only needed his oil remedy in the summer. When fall comes, the nights get cooler. At the first touch of frost, the insects begin to disappear.[10] Just as our valleys have a shelf-life, so do our small, though nagging and exhausting, threats. And the Shepherd, Who anoints us to protect us, walks us through the season until it ends.

But remember, one season is usually replaced with another. Regarding fall, Keller adds, "The foliage on the hills turns to crimson, gold and bronze;

---

10   Keller, 122.

mist and rain begin to fall and the earth prepares for winter."[11] I'm grateful when the draining summer season ends with a cool and beautiful fall. I find the needed respite to handle the winter. I praise God when He anoints me with oil while walking me through a hard season. He does so to strengthen me so I can glorify Him in the winter that may follow.

LORD, DIP ALL OF ME FOR PROTECTION AND HEALING.

Another tweak to our prayers entails asking Jesus to cover all of us with oil, not just our heads. In some countries, dips are built, and the sheep are submerged in the solution—the head repeatedly.[12] Hearing this, I thought of Simon Peter.

The night before His crucifixion, Jesus grabbed a servant's towel to wash His disciples' feet. Either Peter felt he wasn't worthy to have his feet washed by Jesus, or he believed it was beneath Jesus to assume that role. Regardless, Peter refuses Jesus' offer in John 13:8: "You shall never wash my feet!"

Jesus later explained His reason for washing His disciples' feet (vs. 12-19). He wanted His disciples to follow His lead in humility by serving others. When Jesus tells Peter he can't follow Him unless he lets Him wash his feet, Peter asks Jesus to wash his hands and head, too.

In some way, I'm where Peter was. I want to say, "Jesus, I can't keep following You if You only anoint my head. I need You to dip me completely for healing from what I've experienced. And I need Your protection for what's to come. Cover me today. Let me follow You, knowing You are covering me with Your presence."

GOD, REMIND ME THAT "I HAVE THEE, OH, I HAVE THEE."

Bertha Smith's honesty is refreshing. After working through 2 Corinthians 9:8 and after experiencing the load-lifting benefits from this single verse, she

11   Ibid.
12   Ibid, 119.

wrote, "What a sentence! You may be sure that by the time that I had worked on this verse for two weeks, it had come alive for me. Such a victorious, abundant life should only be the normal life for one in whom Christ himself was actually living his own life. Shame on me that at times afterwards I forgot that magnificent truth![13]

What beautiful and helpful transparency. She needed to be reminded of the assuring truth: "I have Thee. Oh, I have Thee." We all need to be reminded of this because we all experience what I call "situational amnesia."

Surprised by a situation too broken to fix, too complicated to figure out, and too demanding to endure, we forget the One Who is with us. We forget having the Spirit of Almighty God within us. Nothing is too complicated for the Creator of the universe. Nothing is too broken for Him to fix, too taxing for Him to endure, or too intimidating to Him. But sometimes, the immediate panic of what's before us causes us to forget who resides in us.

When surprised by an imposing fear, our conditioned response should be prayer—specifically praying, "I have Thee. Oh, I have Thee." For that to be our response, those words should be our prayer and praise every day.

SEEING LIFE AS A MARATHON

David died at seventy (see 2 Samuel 5:4; 1 Kings 2:11). Psalms 57 and 142 remind us that David was a fugitive for fifteen years before he wore the crown. David penned Psalm 23 after reflecting on his life with God. He tended sheep, defeated Goliath, led Israel to defeat the Philistines, was a fugitive from Saul, was nearly captured by the Philistines, acted as a warrior for the Philistines, became king of Israel, sinned with Bathsheba, was driven from Jerusalem by his son Absalom, defeated Absalom and returned as king, identified Solomon as his successor, and raised supplies for building the temple.

Thinking of life as a marathon, I reflected on my Monument 10K race with John Mark. I didn't realize at the start that sponsors offered cups of water

---

13   Smith, 8.

throughout the race. John Mark pointed them out to me. Soon, I conditioned my eyes to look for them.

Three or four times, I told John Mark I needed to stop and walk a while. With encouraging eyes, he said, "Sure." I knew he only stopped for me, so I encouraged him, "Go on, Son. I'm holding you back. Run your race." After saying this to him several times, John Mark, said, "No, Dad, I want to run the race with you."

We completed the race, but I went to bed while John Mark stayed and enjoyed the festivities surrounding the race. Three weeks later, he asked if I wanted to run a marathon with him. I immediately said, "No way." But then, I saw the photographs.

Photographers had lined the road during our race. Some captured John Mark and me running together. I didn't relive the strain and fatigue as much as I did the joy of running the race with my son—having him with me, encouraging me with "Come on, Dad, we're almost there."

Savoring the experience with John Mark, I changed my mind when he asked again and said, "I'd like that, Son." Will I like the training or the feeling of wanting to quit? No. But I wouldn't want to miss the experience of running again with my son.

As David reflected on his life with God, he realized it had been a marathon. The Father conditioned his eyes to the accessible cup and healing oil and gave him everything he needed to continue the race. But David's delight was not in what he had accomplished. We don't hear him list his accomplishments. He never mentioned defeating Goliath or becoming king. His psalm is a praise. He's in awe over his experiences with God—the One Who had stayed with him throughout his life's race.

David's experiences gave him the confidence to follow God from one challenge to the next. Ours will do the same for us.

CHAPTER TEN

REMIND ME OF HOME: I NEED ENCOURAGEMENT!

Surely goodness and mercy shall follow me All the days of my life;
And I will dwell in the house of the Lord Forever.

—Psalm 23:6

ALTHOUGH IT HAPPENED IN 1968, it makes all of us who fly cringe. The wheels on a plane bound for New York did not engage. The pilot informed the passengers that airport personnel were foaming the runway. Calm flight attendants gave instructions on grabbing your ankles and putting your head between your knees. Still, crying and occasional screams echoed throughout the cabin.

Then, the melodic voice of the pilot seeped through the speakers: "We are beginning our final descent. At this moment, in accordance with International Aviation Codes established at Geneva, it is my obligation to inform you that if you believe in God, you should commence prayer."[1] More than likely, most were already praying.

If scholars are right and David prayed this as an older king, he does so with his final descent in mind. He may be ten years or ten days away from death, but verse six sounds as if he was praying with the end in mind.

---

1   Charles R Swindoll, *Encourage Me: Caring Words for Heavy Hearts* (Portland: Multnomah Press, 1982), 41.

Prayer should look backward and forward. In his final years, David reflected on God's goodness and mercy to him, but he also looked forward as he thought about living in the house of the Lord forever.

None of us know when our final descent will be, but we can all benefit from praying as David did. We are encouraged by looking back on God's faithfulness and forward to being at home with Him.

LOOKING BACK

I laugh, hearing the story of a little boy learning Psalm 23 and telling his parents, "I don't like it."

"Don't like what?" his parents asked.

"I don't like having three women follow me."

"What three women?" they pressed.

The boy growled, "Shirley, Gladys, and Mary."

Using "surely" not "Shirley," David employs a Hebrew participle conveying his praise and gratitude to God. He knows "surely," or, literally, "only" God's goodness and lovingkindness will follow Him all his life.[2] David knew this because that's what he experienced with God as his Shepherd.

The word "goodness" describes God's nature. Jesus says no one is good but God (Mark 10:18).[3] "Mercy" points to God's nature in action and means "God's lovingkindness." The word is also found in Hosea, where it describes Hosea's faithful love (lovingkindness) for his wayward wife and how he pursued and restored her after her mistakes.[4]

Knowing this about God's goodness and mercy, scholar John Phillips says God's goodness takes care of *our steps* and His mercy *our stumbles*.[5] His goodness takes us on paths against our nature—paths that show His glory to us and others. Those paths can also drain us. By His goodness, God makes

2   Daniel, 93.
3   This is response to the rich young ruler calling Jesus "good teacher." Jesus' full response to him is, "Why do you call Me good?" Jesus asked him. "No one is good but One—God."
4   Daniel, 93.
5   Phillips, 179.

us lie down when we need to rest or leads us to water (Himself) when we need strength.

We see God's mercy in His staff and oil. God's mercy pulls us back when we go astray and lifts us when we fall. His mercy pours oil on wounds caused by our sin. God's persistent goodness and mercy in our past enable us to press on with Him, trusting Him with an uncertain future

Reviewing Psalm 23, David trusts God's future care by recalling God's history with him. David thanks God for the following:

- Making him lie down for rest—to digest Who God is and all that's happening around him;
- Leading him to waters for strength—when sapped from the journey with God;
- Restoring his being with hope—when circumstances left him hopeless;
- Guiding him on the right paths—even paths he didn't understand or want left him in awe of God;
- Comforting him in hard valleys—God never left his side, even when the frightening "what ifs" came true;
- Constantly healing, protecting, and providing for him—David never felt abandoned by God, though he was often overwhelmed when following Him.

David projects his future with God: "Just as I've experienced in my past, God's goodness and mercy will be with me the rest of my life, not because I earned or deserved it but because God is good." Because he has experienced God's goodness and because he knows God's nature is unchangeable, David rests in his future with God.

Loree created a game called "The Grateful Game" to play with our grandchildren. The rules are simple. At bedtime, everyone takes turns saying, "I'm grateful to God for . . . " Loree and I played the game one night during a stressful season. I had spent two weeks taking my mom to see various doctors. Loree was taking her mom twice a day for radiation treatments. We met each other in bed each night exhausted—and it wasn't even our bed. We were fourteen hundred miles from home in my mom's guest room, still consumed with demands we had left behind.

Loree hoped the game would help our grandkids go to sleep. Playing it did the opposite for us. The more we recognized God's goodness, the more alive we became. No longer dreading what tomorrow held, we were invigorated by all God had done.

A few days later, Loree broke her own rule. She couldn't wait until evening. Consumed by the day before her, she said, "I need to play the game— now!" Back and forth, we listed God's goodness—past and present. We wept together, describing how good God had been. Weight was lifted. Joy surfaced. Delight erupted—all from remembering and thanking God for His goodness.

I find myself repeating Ecclesiastes 1:9 a lot: "There is nothing new under the sun." We may feel life is heavy now, but weariness has always been a part of life. God's goodness and mercy have always been constants, too. We often let what's heavy blind us to our history of God's goodness and mercy. A simple "Grateful Game" can do amazing things for our perspective. I hate to tell Loree, but David created it first.

LOOKING FORWARD TO

Assured of God's goodness and mercy in his remaining days, David described what excited him about his future. When David speaks of dwelling in the house of the Lord forever, I can't decide if he writes this with a sigh of gratitude or a punch of anticipation.

MORE INTIMACY WITH GOD

Scholars offer two positions on what David means. Both are exciting. When we read other psalms by David, he shares his desire to be in God's house and courts. These psalms convey the idea of constantly being at God's tabernacle or temple and involved in God's service. Perhaps David meant this. But since David was a king and not a priest, that interpretation seems impossible. Rather, David expressed his longing to continually experience God's presence as he did in worship and life. He looked forward to those indescribable moments of intimacy with God.[6]

Since few have lived like David, I wonder if we understand the kind of intimacy with God he had and wanted.

An article was written on the tenth anniversary of the release of twenty-three South Korean believers held captive by the Taliban. Sometime after their release, members of the group came to the pastor who was abducted with them. They asked him, "Pastor, don't you wish you were still imprisoned by the Taliban?" The pastor said, "They tell me, 'When I was surrounded by these soldiers, I felt the presence of Jesus in there with me. Now that we are back in Seoul, I am trying to experience that intimacy with Him but I can't. I fast and I pray and I don't feel it. I would rather be back there because of the intimacy I had with him.'"[7]

I believe David experienced that type of intimacy with God and pined to experience it constantly. It enabled him to trash-talk Goliath, praise God as a fugitive in the cave of Adullam, recover from a sinful low-point, survive the hostile take-over by his son Absalom, and finish his life faithfully with God. David experienced it, like the followers from South Korea, in moments of extreme dependence on God. Dependence and intimacy go hand in hand.

BEING HOME WITH GOD

David looked forward to intimacy with God not only on earth but also in heaven.[8] Phillip Keller reminds us David writes this psalm picturing

---

6   Barnes, 213–214.
7   Mark Ellis, "Francis Chan: Korean Missionaries Wish They Were Still Imprisoned by Taliban," Godreports, June 9, 2017, https://www.godreports.com/2017/06/francis-chan-korean-missionaries-wish-they-were-still-imprisoned-by-taliban
8   Wiersbe, 138-139.

God as his Shepherd. And as a former shepherd, David knew the shepherd's responsibility to prepare the pen for his sheep.[9]

The day before His crucifixion, Jesus talked like a shepherd when He spoke of preparing a place for His sheep: "Let not your heart be troubled; you believe in God, believe also in Me. In My Father's house are many mansions; if *it were* not *so*, I would have told you. I go to prepare a place for you. And if I go and prepare a place for you, I will come again and receive you to Myself; that where I am, *there* you may be also" (John 14:1-3).

Revelation 21 gives us a picture of the pen Jesus is preparing. John describes Heaven with four walls surrounding it, each standing twenty stories tall and made of jasper (v. 18). They are supported by twelve foundations, each comprised of precious gems (vs. 19-20). Each wall hosts three gates, and each gate is cut from a single pearl (vs. 10-14, 21).

In heaven, we are safe (vv. 25–27). The different sounds confirm it. No sirens or sobs from death and pain are heard (vv. 3-4). The streets and facilities are made of transparent gold (v. 18). No night exists in heaven because the glory of God reflects off these (v. 23).

Although David did not have the picture provided in Revelation 21, the thought of being finished on earth and being in God's presence in Heaven motivated his faithfulness to the end. It often motivates me as well.

As fatigue set in toward the end of my run with my son, I began looking at mile markers. Knowing ten kilometers means 6.2 miles, I saw mile marker four and thought, *Just two more miles.* At this point, someone posted a sign saying, "You're almost home." Then about half a mile out, I saw the huge banner in the distance: "Finish Line!" Focusing on it, I said to myself, "Come on, Mark; you're almost there. Finish strong!"

That's what Jesus' promise of Heaven does for us. Life on earth is a wink of time compared to eternity with Him. Knowing this, we press on with our Good Shepherd on unnatural paths and in unwanted valleys. We picture

---

9   Keller, 137.

Heaven, saying, "Keep running your race with Jesus. Finish strong. You're almost home."

ENCOURAGING PRAYER

My son's presence beside me was invaluable—not only in running the race but also in finishing strong. Studying Psalm 23 describes all we gain from having Jesus with us as our Good Shepherd. Even though we don't see Him physically beside us, Jesus promises His presence within us as the Holy Spirit. The night before His crucifixion, Jesus told His disciples, "If you love Me, keep My commandments. And I will pray the Father, and He will give you another Helper, that He may abide with you forever—the Spirit of truth, whom the world cannot receive, because it neither sees Him nor knows Him; but you know Him, for He dwells with you and will be in you. I will not leave you orphans; I will come to you" (John 14:15–18).

"Counselor" or "Helper" is a compound Greek word that means "called to your side." The verb form is translated elsewhere in Scripture as "encourage." The Holy Spirit is the presence of Jesus within us, encouraging us as we follow Him. One of the ways He inspires us to follow is through timely reminders. When praying, we should ask Him to remind us of some things.

GOD'S PAST GOODNESS AND MERCY

In John 16:13, Jesus promises that the Spirit will guide us in all truth. That includes the truth about how He led us with goodness and mercy in our past. Regarding God's goodness and mercy, Warren Wiersbe writes, "The things that perplex and disturb us today will all be clear when we get to heaven. We will look back and see 'only goodness and mercy.'"[10] Gratefully, we don't have to wait until Heaven to look back and see it.

When in middle school, my sons frequently danced on their mom's last frayed nerve. My brother and I did the same to our mom. Knowing this, I

---

10 Wiersbe, 138.

asked Mom to describe to Loree how my brother and I made life difficult for her. I wanted Loree to know her current season with our sons was hard, but she would survive. Surprisingly, Mom didn't remember it that way. She told Loree how good those years were. In that moment, I thought, *God gives moms the gift of divine amnesia.* He does the same for us, allowing us to remember His goodness and mercy through all the challenging paths or low valleys.

Since that's where we end, why not start there? We should ask the Holy Spirit to remind us of His goodness and mercy throughout our life with Him. We don't have to wait until later to enjoy it. This will inspire us to finish strong.

THE BEAUTY AND POWER OF INTIMACY WITH GOD

The article on the Taliban abductees also provided a conversation with Reverend Eric Foley, CEO and co-founder of Voice of the Martyrs Korea, and his wife, Dr. Hyun Sook Foley. The couple described the beauty and strength of Jesus' followers in North Korea.

North Korea is ranked first on Open Door USA's *World Watch List* of countries where being a believer is most difficult. Believers there have a different perspective of their plight than followers in South Korea or America.

Talking with a believer who defected from North Korea, Dr. Foley asked him how to pray for him. He answered, "You pray for us? We pray for you! That's the problem with you American Christians and South Korean Christians! You have so much, you put your faith in your money and in your freedom. In North Korea we have neither money nor freedom, but we have Christ and we've found He's sufficient."[11]

David experienced the same intimacy with God as this North Korean follower. David opened Psalm 23 by proclaiming that the Lord was his Shepherd, and he ended it by saying he would "dwell in the house of the LORD forever." On both occasions, the word translated *Lord* is "Yahweh—The Great I AM!" It's the relational side of God and conveys His desire and our opportunity to experience intimacy with Him. From that intimacy, we are filled with awe and strength. Both are needed to follow Him gratefully and confidently until He calls us home.

As David and the follower from North Korea pointed out, "sufficiency" and "intimacy" go hand in hand. When our sufficiency in life is tied to anything or anyone other than Jesus, it robs us of our intimacy with Him. When it is in Jesus alone, we know the beauty and strength God intended from being intimately close to Him.

Pray the following: "Holy Spirit, show me if my sufficiency in life is in anyone or anything else. Help me see my sufficiency is in Jesus alone. Help me know again the beauty and power of intimacy with Jesus."

OUR PROMISE OF HOME

One of the benefits of seeing Jesus as our Good Shepherd is being reminded of the pen He prepares for His sheep.[12] First-century shepherds often prepared pens comprised of stones and fallen branches. They had only one opening. As the shepherd led the sheep through, he lay across it at night to secure them.[13]

Jesus was familiar with this practice. In John 10:7–10, Jesus describes Himself as the Door of the sheep. That also makes His promise in John 14:1–3 personal. All followers get to experience Heaven together. But He also promises that we all get to be with Him in Heaven.

Home is not so much where we live, but who we are with. We should ask the Spirit to remind us of Jesus' promise about the relationships we'll enjoy in heaven. Not only will we experience reunions with family and friends, but we will also get to see Moses, Elijah, Peter, Paul, David, and, most importantly, Jesus. This should encourage us to continue following Him.

---

12   William Barclay, *The Gospel of John, Revised Edition* (Philadelphia: The Westminster Press, 1975), 58.
13   F. F. Bruce, *The Gospel of John* (Grand Rapids: William B. Eerdmans Publishing Company, 1983), 224.

A GREAT TRIBUTE

In his book on David, Chuck Swindoll provides a helpful exercise. He first points the reader to Acts 13:36: "For David, after he had served his own generation by the will of God, fell asleep, was buried with his fathers, and saw corruption."

Swindoll then instructs the reader to consider using this same verse for personal inspiration. Instead of placing David's name in the verse, Swindoll says, "Insert your own." Listen to how it sounds: "For _____ (your name), after he/she served the purpose of God in his/her generation, fell asleep, and was buried and passed away from the face of the earth."[14]

David finished strong for the following reasons:

- God, Who had shepherded David thus far, would continue to the end. God had already proven He would not change His nature, regardless of what David faced.
- David had experienced intimacy with God, which carried him over the hard paths and through the deep valleys. Nothing was more beautiful and powerful to him than his intimacy with God.
- David knew this life was short compared to eternity with God. He wanted to finish strong, knowing his time on earth was limited.
- David wanted to know he had fulfilled God's purpose for his life in his generation.

I know following Jesus can be hard. That's why God preserved David's psalm. It remains in Scripture to inspire us to follow Jesus faithfully and dependently to the end.

---

14 Charles R. Swindoll, *David: A Man of Passion & Destiny* (Dallas: Word Publishing, 1997), 284-85.

WORKS CITED

Allen, Charles L. *God's Psychiatry*. Reprinted. New York: Jove/HBJ Books. 1978.

Bainton, Roland. *Here I Stand: A Life of Martin Luther*. New York: Abingdon Press, 1950.

Barclay, William. *The Gospel of John, Revised Edition*. Philadelphia: The Westminster Press. 1975.

Barnes, Albert. *Notes on the Old Testament: Psalms, Volume 1*. Grand Rapids, Michigan: Baker Book House. 1870-72.

Bratcher, Robert G. and William D. Reyburn. *UBS Old Testament Handbook Series: The Book of Psalm*. United Bible Societies. 1978-2004. Biblesoft PC Study Bible One Touch Professional Series.

Brown, Francis. Cooperation by S. R. Driver and Charles A. Briggs. *The New Brown–Driver–Briggs–Genesis Hebrew and English Lexicon*. Peabody, Massachusetts: Hendrickson Publishers. 1979.

Bruce, F. F. *The Gospel of John*. Grand Rapids, Michigan: William B. Eerdmans Publishing Company. 1983.

Crabtree, Shona. "Book Uncovers a Lonely, Spiritually Desolate Mother Teresa." *Christianity Today* online. August 30, 2007, http://www.christianitytoday. com/ct/2007/augustweb-only/135-43.0.html.

Daniel, Robert T. *How to Study the Psalms.* Westwood, New Jersey: Fleming H. Revell Company, 195.

DePree, Max. *Leadership Is an Art.* New York: Dell Publishing. 1989.

Ellis, Mark. "Francis Chan: Korean Missionaries Wish They Were Still Imprisoned by Taliban." *Godreports* online. June 9, 2017. https://www. godreports.com/2017/06/francis-chan-korean-missionaries-wish-they-were-still-imprisoned-by-taliban.

Ellsworth Day, Richard, *The Shadow of the Broad Brim: The Life Story of Charles Haddon Spurgeon Heir of the Puritans.* Philadelphia; The Judson Press. 1934.

Evans, Tony, *Praying Through the Names of God.* Eugene, Oregon: Harvest House Publishers. 2014.

Evans, Tony. *The Power of God's Names.* Eugen: Harvest House Publishers. 2014.

Falwell, Macel. *Jerry Falwell: His Life and Legacy.* New York: Howard Books. 2008.

Goodreads. "Surprised by Joy Quotes." https://www.goodreads.com/work/ quotes/877675-surprised-by-joy-the-shape-of-my-early-life.

Groopman, Jerome. *The Anatomy of Hope: How People Prevail in the Face of Illness.* New York: Random House. 2004.

Jacob, Edmond. *Theology of the Old Testament.* Trans. by Arthur W. Heathcote and Philip J. Allcock. New York: Harper & Brothers Publishers, 195.

Kaiser, Walter C. Jr., Garrett, Duane A. *NIV Archaeological Study Bible* (Grand Rapids, Michigan: Zondervan, 2005), 395.

Keller, Phillip. *A Shepherd Looks at Psalm 23*. Minneapolis, Minnesota: World Wide Publications. 1970.

Keller, Timothy. "Timothy Keller@HKU--Hope Beyond the Walls of the World." https://www.youtube.com/watch?v=SD5LYJ3us0U.

Leupold, H. C. *Exposition of the Psalms*. Columbus: The Wartburg Press. 1959.

Lockyer, Herbert. *All the Trades and Occupations of the Bible*. Grand Rapids: Zondervan. 1969.

Long, Thomas G. *Preaching and the Literary Forms of the Bible*. Philadelphia: Fortress Press. 1989.

McCasland, David. Compiler and Editor. *The Quotable Oswald Chambers*. Grand Rapids: Discovery House. 2008.

Meyer, F. B. *Great Men of the Bible, Vol. 2*. Grand Rapids, Michigan: Zondervan. 1982.

"Missionary Biographies: Adoniram Judson, A Baptist Page Portrait." The Baptist Page. 1997-2001. http://www.wholesomewords.org/missions/ bjudson20.html.

Morgan, G. Campbell. *Great Chapters of the Bible*. Old Tappan, New Jersey: Fleming H. Revell Company. 1935.

Morgan, G. Campbell. *Notes on the Psalms*. Old Tappan: Fleming H. Revell. 1947.

Oxford English and Spanish Dictionary, Synonyms, and Spanish to English Translator. Oxford Lexico. Accessed May 1, 2022. https://en.oxforddictionaries.com/ definition/dependent.

Peale, Norman Vincent. *The Rewards of Positive Living*. 1981.

Phillips, John. *Exploring the Psalms: Psalms 1-88*. Neptune: Loizeaux Brothers. 1988.

Pink, Arthur. *The Attributes of God*. Grand Rapids: Baker Book House. 1975.

Platt, David. "Meditating on God's Presence." 1:00:22, June 29, 2014, https://radical.net/message/meditating-on-gods-presence.

Sanders, J. Oswald. *Spiritual Leadership: Principles of Excellence for Every Believer*. Second Revision. Chicago: Moody Press. 1994.

Schoenian, Susan. "Sheep 201: A Beginner's Guide to Raising Sheep." Sheep 201. April 19, 2021. http://www.sheep101.info/201/behavior.html.

Smith, Bertha. *Go Home and Tell*. Nashville: Broadman Press. 1965.

Spurgeon, Charles Haddon. *Psalms*. Grand Rapids: Kregel Publications. 1968.

Stott, John. *Favorite Psalms*. Chicago: Moody Press. 1988.

Swindoll, Charles R. *David: A Man of Passion & Destiny*. Dallas: Word Publishing. 1997.

Swindoll, Charles R. *Encourage Me: Caring Words for Heavy Hearts*. Portland: Multnomah Press. 1982.

Swindoll, Charles R. *Strengthening Your Grip*. Waco: Word Books. 1982.

Swindoll, Charles R. *Three Steps Forward Two Steps Back: Persevering through Pressure*. Nashville: Thomas Nelson Publishers. 1980.

Strong, James. *New Exhaustive Strong's Numbers and Concordance with Expanded Greek-Hebrew Dictionary*. Nashville, Tennessee: Thomas Nelson, 2003. Biblesoft PC Study Bible One Touch Professional Series.

Tierney, John. "Do You Suffer from Decision Fatigue?" *The New York Times Magazine.* August 17, 2011. http://www.nytimes.com/2011/08/21/magazine/do-you-suffer-from-decision-fatigue.html?mcubz=0.

Wiersbe, Warren W. *The Bible Exposition Commentary, Old Testament, Wisdom and Poetry, Job-Song of Solomon.* Colorado Springs: David C. Cook. 2004.

Yates, Kyle M. *Studies in Psalms.* Nashville: Broadman Press. 1953.

For more information about
Mark Becton
and

Praying with David
please connect at:

Twitter: @BectonMark

Ambassador International's mission is to magnify the Lord Jesus Christ
and promote His gospel through the written word.

We believe through the publication of Christian literature, Jesus Christ and
His Word will be exalted, believers will be strengthened in their walk with

Him, and the lost will be directed to Jesus Christ as the only way of salvation.

For more information about
AMBASSADOR INTERNATIONAL
please connect at:

www.ambassador-international.com

*Thank you for reading this book. Please consider leaving us a
review on your social media, favorite retailer's website,
Goodreads or Bookbub, or our website.*

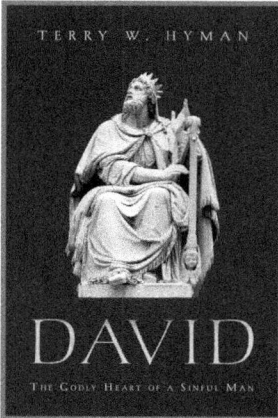

To some people, saying David had a godly heart is almost offensive. How do you apply that description to a man whose legacy includes neglecting responsibilities, lust, adultery, murder, deception, hypocrisy, and callous indifference? *David: The Godly Heart of a Sinful Man* examines David's heart, identifying specific character qualities that influenced his response when confronted with his sin.

Job, the book and the man, is well-known even in the public arena. However, the main character of the book is the Triune God. Moreover, some have suggested that the book of Job focuses on the larger problem of evil in a good God's world. By definition that would include the concept of victimhood. However, Dr. Jim Halla thinks that approach misses major issues. *The Book of Job: God's Faithfulness in Troubled Times* presents an in depth look into Job and how it applies to the New Testament, Jesus, and us.

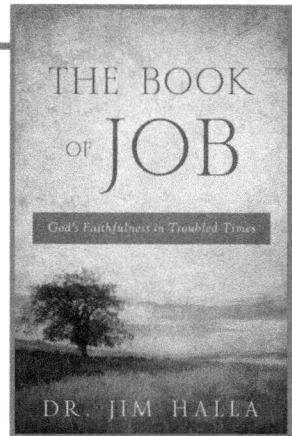

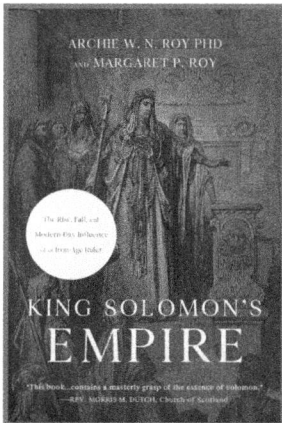

King Solomon is known as the wisest and richest man to have ever lived, but who was this man really? Even though we read his words in the Bible, this man who was the son of "the man after God's own heart" remains a mystery to this day. Even his death is veiled in conspiracy theories. How could a man who was granted his greatest wish by God Himself be so enamored with the pleasures of this world—hungry for sex, power, and more wealth? In *King Solomon's Empire*, Archie and Margaret Roy take an in-depth look into the life of the wise king and the kingdom he led.

www.ingramcontent.com/pod-product-compliance
Lightning Source LLC
Chambersburg PA
CBHW071820090426
42737CB00012B/2150